WHAT BROTHERS ARE SAY[ING]
TOGETHER IN CHR[IST]

"Victor Knowles has been one of my heroes for decades. But in his timely and powerful new volume, *Together in Christ,* Victor is at his very best. Here he thoroughly excavates the massive foundation of Christian unity—which lies as bedrock all through Scripture, undergirding the hopes of key Christian leaders across the centuries. He reawakens current hopes as well—reminding today's Christians that something that is of such paramount importance to God must never be dismissed as an *impossible* dream. Finally, Knowles offers some simple but powerful steps toward Christian unity. If I were pope, this book would be required reading for every Christian leader! I am triple-blessed by this book and hope it gets maximum circulation."

> **— LYNN ANDERSON, President,**
> **Hope Network Ministries, San Antonio, Texas**

"Few in our movement have committed themselves to the cause of unity like Victor Knowles. I am thankful for his unwavering conviction that Jesus' prayer is 'mission possible' and welcome this needed reminder to be the one body of Christ!"

> **— RICK ATCHLEY, Preaching Minister,**
> **Richland Hills Church of Christ, N. Richland Hills, Texas**

"A very comprehensive, well-researched and documented treatment of the always relevant theme of unity—probably the most thorough, insightful book on this subject you will find anywhere. Each chapter is interspersed with many fascinating personal experiences that illustrate the points the author is making. Some plans for a practical implementation of the plea for unity are given for consideration in the epilogue."

> **— HARVEY C. BREAM, JR., Teaching Minister,**
> **Bright Christian Church, Lawrenceburg, Indiana**

"This book has a keenness of pen for which Victor Knowles is known. The book's theme and goal is unity, but it still comes across that we would be better divided by the truth than united by error. It puts the emphasis on unity in the essentials rather than unity for its own sake. The reader will thrill to see what the Scriptures have said, the slogans have encouraged, the songwriters and poets have written, along with the insights that Victor and his brethren, both living and dead, have written on this important subject."

> **— GEORGE L. FAULL, President,**
> **Summit Theological Seminary, Peru, Indiana**

"Unity. Scripture describes it. Emotion desires it. Common sense requires it. Jesus prayed for it. The Holy Spirit brings it. Believers who have tasted it will long for more. I thank the Lord for His servants like Victor Knowles who steadily remind us to 'keep the unity of the Spirit in the bond of peace.' This book truly encourages us to come *together in Christ*."

**— DAVID FAUST, President,
Cincinnati Christian University, Cincinnati, Ohio**

"Victor Knowles has given his life to the healing of fractures in the visible unity of Christ's body. In *Together in Christ* he provides a rich resource for inspiration and courage to live out the truth of Ephesians 4:4, 'There is one body.' Knowles' powerful call to unity through Scriptures, prayers, songs and documents will surely shape the hearts and minds of readers so that God's gift of unity becomes *more than a dream*. We cannot afford to ignore that call, for it has profound implications for our churches and for our lives as Christians."

**— DOUGLAS A. FOSTER, Director, Center for Restoration Studies,
Abilene Christian University, Abilene, Texas**

"For two decades Victor Knowles has consistently sounded the trumpet and waved the banner among Christian Churches and Churches of Christ to rally us around the cause of Christian unity. Because of his passion for and faithfulness to God's calling to make us one, no contemporary leader among us deserves a hearing more on the subject *together in Christ*. Two words describe this timely book— biblical and devotional. Every unity text in the two testaments of Scripture is documented. The impact of the word of God is further quickened to our hearts by the record of hymns, songs, poetry, prayers, and statements from respected leaders. If you read only one book on Christian unity this year (and you should, especially this year), this should be the one."

**— KEN IDLEMAN, President,
Ozark Christian College, Joplin, Missouri**

"*Together in Christ* is a valuable resource for the serious student of Christian unity. It traces the biblical and historical roots of unity and includes numerous quotes from some of the finest minds in our divided journey. The book contains a wealth of information on all of the efforts which have been made to produce unity in a global context, and yet it refrains from giving the reader pat answers. Rather, it focuses on the centrality of Christ as our point of unity and it creates hope that unity can be achieved for the purpose of fulfilling the mission of our Lord. I highly recommend it for all those who care deeply about unity. I will keep my copy of this book close at hand."

**— BRYCE JESSUP, President,
William Jessup University, Rocklin, California**

"Another good work from Victor Knowles' prolific and creative pen. We always know that what Victor writes will penetrate to the heart and move the soul. But this book is special, grounded in Scripture and canvassing as it does the great landscape of unity thought among the heirs of the Stone-Campbell movement. All of it is good, but the final two chapters, freshly outlining an appeal for our marching together, is perhaps the best of the book. One can enjoy it for browsing, for careful reading, or for reference."

— **THOMAS A. LANGFORD, professor emeritus,**
Texas Tech University, Lubbock, Texas

"*Together in Christ* is a book long overdue—comprehensive, convicting, compelling—that opens the heart of its author to reveal his passion to see all believers united in one body."

— **MARSHALL LEGGETT, Chancellor,**
Milligan College, Milligan College, Tennessee

"We are forced to believe, in the light of our Lord's prayer in John 17:21, that our failure to evangelize the world is due largely to the lack of unity among Christians. Victor Knowles, with his usual passion for unity, does a magnificent job of making all of God's people aware of their responsibility in this matter. The first two chapters alone will be used over and over by the serious student of the body of Christ. *Together in Christ* should be in every Christian home and on every minister's desk. It's a great book and I'm glad to recommend it."

— **BEN MEROLD, Senior Minister,**
Harvester Christian Church, St. Charles, Missouri

"Victor hits the nail on the head in *Together in Christ*. His experience in unity meetings plus his strong grasp of Scripture makes him just the man to write this book. I hope every church leader will read this book. It will penetrate your heart with the truth of the message and the passion for reuniting God's fragmented people. Well done, Victor!"

— **MARVIN PHILLIPS, Director,**
Marvin Phillips Ministries, Tulsa, Oklahoma

"Reminders of the Savior's plea for His beloved followers to acknowledge their status as one body in Him are needed: frequently . . . pointedly . . . lovingly. The compendium of biblical texts, historical data, and other prompts to unity that Victor Knowles has produced is a welcome gift at a promising moment."

— **RUBEL SHELLY, Adjunct Professor,**
Rochester College, Rochester Hills, Michigan

"*Together in Christ* is a masterpiece on Christian unity that should be in the library and life (from the shelves to the souls) of every Bible-believing church. It deals with the what, why, and how of Christian unity and can be summarized with 'unity is not ours to manufacture, but is ours to maintain.' Each separate chapter is worth the price of the book. Never before has such an anthology of classic statements about unity been assembled (88 different people in chapters 7 and 8). Contemporary Christianity, locally and globally, would be transformed to God's intention for the church if members would form small groups to analyze and apply the contents of each chapter. This is a 'must reading and heeding' book."

— KNOFEL STATON, Professor,
Hope International University, Fullerton, California

"Victor Knowles embodies our goal of keeping 'the unity of the Spirit in the bond of peace' as well as anyone I know. This helpful compilation of resources will bless all who seek to restore New Testament Christianity."

— SAM E. STONE, former editor, *Christian Standard*;
author, *Simply Christians*

"Victor Knowles pleads with us to unite in Christ on biblical principles and gives us some practical ways we can do this. *Together in Christ* will encourage you to work harder, study more, do more, and love more for unity in the church. It touches the heart, appeals to the mind, and reaches the soul. Victor keeps Scripture constantly before him with Christ as the focal point. This book urges brothers and sisters in Christ to earnestly work toward greater unity now."

— CALVIN WARPULA, Pulpit Minister,
San Jose Church of Christ, Jacksonville, Florida

TOGETHER IN Christ

TOGETHER IN *Christ*

More than a Dream

VICTOR KNOWLES

LEAFWOOD
PUBLISHERS

COLLEGE PRESS PUBLISHING COMPANY · JOPLIN, MISSOURI

Library of Congress Cataloging-in-Publication Data

Knowles, Victor.
   Together in Christ: more than a dream/by Victor Knowles.
         p. cm.
   ISBN 0-89900-942-5 (softback)
   1. Christian Union.   2. Restoration movement (Christianity).   I. Title.
   BX8.3.K56 1997
   280'.042—dc22

                                                      2006004189

Dedication

To all who have gone before us

bearing the burden, paying the price,

seeking to honor our Lord's prayer,

"That they all may be one."

FOREWORD

Victor Knowles and I share a passion for the history of the American Restoration Movement. Although we were reared and educated in different corners of that heritage, it was inevitable that we would meet one day and find common ground. For the past several years, I have invited Victor to teach classses on Christian unity at the annual Pepperdine University Bible Lectures in Malibu, California. He never fails to inspire his listeners to long for oneness in the body of Christ.

No one encouraged me more when I was researching and writing *Christians on the Oregon Trail: Churches of Christ and Christian Churches in Early Oregon* than Victor Knowles. He not only wrote a beautiful tribute for the back cover, but he provided a grand conclusion to the book with his majestic poem, "O Oregon!"

Victor is the founder and president of POEM (Peace on Earth Ministries), and he has served as the editor of the quarterly magazine, *One Body*, for more than twenty years. These ministries have prepared him well for the compiling of this timely book. For years he has consistently challenged all of us in the Restoration Movement to recognize one another as brothers and sisters in Christ in spite of our differences, and now he has placed in our hands an easy-to-reference manual on Christian unity, a veritable roadmap, to prod us down the "Father's road" toward realizing that dream of oneness.

Prior to reading this book, I would have guessed that "Prayers for Unity" and "Songs of Unity" would be my favorite chapters—and they certainly do soar to sublime heights. But I was unprepared for the powerful imagery in the chapter on "Symbols of Unity." The visual reminder in "The Cross, Baptism, and the Lord's Supper" of our inherent oneness with God and with each other is surely a precious gift that we must never lose.

I warmly recommend this volume to anyone who longs for the fulfillment of John 17:21 in our own day. This book is well conceived, well researched and well written. Readers will find in it a rich blend of Scriptures and stories, songs and prayers, wisdom and humor, insight and challenge. It is no surprise that this book ends with an appeal to the centrality of Christ, the authority of Scripture, the necessity of unity, and the urgency of evangelism. This is vintage Victor Knowles.

Jerry Rushford
Professor of Church History
Pepperdine University
Malibu, California

CONTENTS

Preface **11**

1 — The Father's Road to Unity **13**
Scriptures on Unity

2 — Turning Our Dreams into Prayers **25**
Prayers for Unity

3 — O for a Thousand Christians to Sing! **45**
Songs of Unity

4 — The Cross, Baptism, and the Lord's Supper **59**
Symbols of Unity

5 — "In Essentials, Unity" **73**
Slogans on Unity

6 — The Body That Willed to Die **85**
Documents Advocating Unity

7 — May I Say Something? (Part I) **95**
Statements on Unity

8 — May I Say Something? (Part II) **109**
Statements on Unity

9 — A New Appeal for an Old Ideal (Part I) **123**
A Plea for Unity

10 — A New Appeal for an Old Ideal (Part II) **137**
A Plea for Unity

Epilogue and Poems about Unity **153**

Recommended Reading and Resources **165**

PREFACE

What do most of us do when we attend church? We hear Scripture, God's Holy Word, read. We offer our prayers and petitions to God in Jesus' name. We lift our voices in songs of praise. We partake of the bread and cup, the Lord's Supper. We witness the death, burial, and resurrection of Christ when one confesses His name and is baptized into Christ. We listen to teaching and preaching where the Word of God is explained and proclaimed. We enjoy fellowship with other believers. These are some of the things that help make up our church experience. These are also the very things that make up the chapters of this book.

We will begin where every Christian book should begin—with Scripture. In Chapter One we will travel the Father's road to Christian unity, following a spiritual "Route 66" from Genesis to Revelation.

Chapter Two features great prayers for Christian unity, prayers that are both ancient and modern. Of greatest importance, of course, is Jesus' prayer for our unity in John 17, "That they all may be one . . . that the world may believe."

In Chapter Three we'll examine some of the songs that believers have been singing that exalt unity, some as old as the Old Testament itself. Jesus sang some of these songs from His youth. His church continues singing about unity today.

Biblical symbols of unity is the theme of Chapter Four. We will consider several, but will focus primarily on three of the most significant in the New Testament: the cross, baptism, and the Lord's Supper.

Chapter Five takes a look at some of the most famous slogans that have been coined in the relentless pursuit of Christian unity; slogans like "In essentials, unity; in opinions, liberty; in all things, charity."

We'll examine two historic documents advocating Christian unity in

Chapter Six. These documents, written only a few years apart in the early nineteenth century, helped produce a great unity movement in America. My own roots run deep in this Restoration Movement, sometimes called the Stone-Campbell Movement.

In Chapter Seven and Chapter Eight we will give heed to some significant statements made by others on the theme of unity. These come from spiritual statesmen themselves, and were made in statesmanlike fashion.

Finally, in Chapter Nine and Chapter Ten I will make "A New Appeal for an Old Ideal"—that ideal being that God has always wanted His children to be "together in Christ." Being one in Christ is more than a dream—it is a present-day, absolute living reality.

A word of caution is in order. If you do not believe that Scripture is God's inspired, infallible, authoritative word, this book is not for you. Scripture should be the starting point, not a sticking point.

If you do not believe that Jesus Christ is the Son of the living God, that He was eternal with the Father, born of a virgin, fully God and fully man, lived a sinless life, performed miracles, taught nothing but truth, died an atoning death on the cross, bodily arose from the dead on the third day, ascended into heaven where He intercedes for us, and will return in power and glory to receive us unto Himself, then this book is not for you.

And if you do not believe that Jesus prayed a prayer that is possible to be answered, or that the world for which He died can be evangelized when His people are one, this book is definitely not for you.

But if you are committed to the eternal truth of Holy Scripture, believe in the Christ portrayed in Holy Scripture, and want to honor His dying prayer, then this book is for you.

"Now may the God of patience and comfort grant you to be likeminded toward one another, according to Christ Jesus, that you may with one mind and one mouth glorify the God and Father of our Lord Jesus Christ. Therefore receive one another, just as Christ also received us, to the glory of God" (Rom. 15:5-7).

Victor Knowles

Chapter One

THE FATHER'S ROAD TO UNITY
SCRIPTURES ON UNITY

John Steinbeck, in *The Grapes of Wrath*, called Route 66 the "Mother Road" of the United States. Others have called this famous highway the "Main Street of America." At one time it was one of the most traveled roads in America. Route 66 started in Chicago and ended in Los Angeles, 2,448 miles later. Travelers went through eight states in the process. The road sign markers for Route 66 are now icons. Route 66 often pops up in song lyrics, movies, and memorabilia. Since 1987 I have lived in the Carthage-Joplin area in Missouri, two of the towns that Route 66 once ran through.

There is another Route 66, a spiritual one, which runs from Genesis to Revelation. It is the Father's road to Christian unity. It begins with God in the creation chapter, travels through the Old Testament, climbs the highest peak in Scripture—where the cross of Christ towers over everything and everybody—and comes to an end at the Throne of the Lamb in The Revelation of Jesus Christ.

The Bible itself is a remarkable example of unity. It contains sixty-six books written by forty different authors living on three continents over a span of 1,600 years. Some of these men, coming from all walks of life, never even heard of each other, yet there is no evidence of collusion or collaboration. The Bible not only is a model of unity but models unity and makes an urgent appeal for unity throughout its sacred pages. For all of us to be on the same page on the doctrine of unity, we should begin with the sacred pages of God's Word.

> For all of us to be on the same page on the doctrine of unity, we should begin with the sacred pages of God's Word.

What follows in this chapter are sixty-six selected passages on unity. Twelve of the selections come from the Old Testament, and the rest are taken from the New Testament with over twenty coming from the book of Ephesians, which some have called the "Alps" of the New Testament.

Ladies and gentlemen, start your engines! We are about to travel the Father's road to unity.

1 "In the beginning God created the heavens and the earth" (Gen. 1:1, NIV). The Hebrew word for God (*elohim*) is plural indicating from the outset that God is a unity.

"Then God said, 'Let Us make man in Our image, according to **2** Our likeness . . .' (Gen. 1:26, NASB). The unity of the Godhead is seen when we understand that Christ and the Holy Spirit also participated in the creation of man (Gen. 1:2; Col. 1:16).

3 "For this reason a man will leave his father and mother and be united to his wife, and they will become one flesh" (Gen. 2:24, NIV). The union of a man and a woman in marriage results in the two becoming one. Marriage is a divine unity.

"I will make you into a great nation and I will bless you" (Gen. **4** 12:2, NIV). Through one man (Abraham) and one nation (Israel) God promised to bless all peoples (nations) on earth. God never intended for Israel to be divided into two nations as they eventually did.

5 "So Abram said to Lot, 'Please let there be no strife between you and me, and between my herdsmen and your herdsmen; for we are brethren" (Gen. 13:8, NKJV). This is one of the most heartfelt appeals for unity in the Old Testament.

"Hear O Israel! The LORD is our God, the LORD is one!" (Deut. **6** 6:4). Known as the *Shema*, the oneness of God is exalted. Other nations had a multiplicity of gods; Israel had but one, the LORD.

7 "Now when he had finished speaking to Saul, the soul of Jonathan was knit to the soul of David, and Jonathan loved him as his own soul" (1 Sam. 18:1, NKJV). What a poignant passage! In Christ our souls should also be knit together in love (Col. 2:2).

"So all the men of Israel were gathered against the city, united together as one man" (Judg. 20:11, NKJV). Israel was made up of twelve tribes, but here they rose up as one man. F. LaGard Smith notes that as long as they saw themselves as a part of the larger family, they remained united, strong, and victorious.

9 "I will make them one nation in the land, on the mountains of Israel. There will be one king over all of them and they will never again be two nations or be divided into two kingdoms" (Ezek. 37:22, NIV). After the kingdom divided, God promised a wonderful reunion of Israel and Judah.

"How good and pleasant it is when brothers live together in **10** unity! It is like precious oil poured on the head, running down on the beard, running down on Aaron's beard, down on the collar of his robes. It is as if the dew of Hermon were falling on Mount Zion. For there the LORD bestows his blessing, even life forevermore" (Ps. 133:1-3, NIV). God bestows His blessing where unity prevails. Is it possible He withholds or even withdraws His blessing where division reigns?

> How good and pleasant it is when brothers live together in unity!

11 "These six things the LORD hates, Yes, seven are an abomination to Him: A proud look, A lying tongue, Hands that shed innocent blood, A heart that devises wicked plans, Feet that are swift in running to evil, A false witness who speaks lies, And one who sows discord among brethren." (Prov. 6:16-19, NKJV). God hates these six things but the seventh is an absolute "abomination" to Him. "Abomination" is the strongest word used in Scripture to express God's hatred for sin. Those who "sow discord among brethren" are under God's anathema!

"Two are better than one, because they have a good reward **12** for their toil. For if they fall, one will lift up his fellow. But woe to him who is alone when he falls and has not another to lift him up! Again, if two lie together, they keep warm, but how can one keep warm alone? And though a man might prevail against one who is alone, two will withstand him—a threefold cord is not quickly broken" (Eccl. 4:9-12, ESV).

Scripture

13 "Every kingdom divided against itself will be ruined, and every city or household divided against itself will not stand" (Matt. 12:25, NIV). This would also be true of the spiritual household of God, the church. When we take our stand together in Christ, we will never be divided.

"So then, they are no longer two but one flesh. Therefore what God has joined together, let not man separate" (Matt. 19:6, NKJV). Jesus taught that marriage is a divine union between a man and a woman that should never be dissolved. God is the spiritual glue that binds them together in love. Thus, marriage is a "holy triangle" with living lines of love flowing between God, husband, and wife. **14**

15 "And I have other sheep, which are not of this fold; I must bring them also, and they shall hear My voice; and they shall become one flock with one shepherd" (John 10:16, NASB). Please notice the powerful urgency and positive expectancy of Jesus in this prophetic declaration of unity.

"I and My Father are one" (John 10:30, NKJV). The wonderful unity of the Father and Son is seen in this passage. Jesus and the Father are one in name (Jehovah/Lord) one in nature (divine), one in enjoyment (fellowship), and one in purpose (the redemption of fallen man). **16**

17 "A new command I give you: Love one another. As I have loved you, so you must love one another. By this all men will know that you are my disciples, if you love one another" (John 13:34,35, NIV). Love is an act of the will. The true Christian will love all fellow believers just as Christ loves him—unconditionally, constantly, to the very end.

"Holy Father, keep through Your name those whom You have given Me, that they may be one as We are" (John 17:11, NKJV). On the night He was betrayed, Jesus prayed for the unity of His disciples. The pact of unity would help them impact the world. **18**

19 "I do not pray for these alone, but also for those who will believe in Me through their word; that they all may be one, as You, Father, are in Me, and I in You; that they also may be one in Us, that the world may believe that You sent Me" (John 17:20,21, NKJV). Jesus prayed for a unity among future believers that was based upon Christ-centered apostolic teaching; a unity that was modeled by the Father and Son, resulting in nonbelievers coming to faith in Him.

"And the glory which You gave Me I have given them, that they **20** may be one just as We are one: I in them, and You in Me; that they may be made perfect in one, and that the world may know that You have sent Me, and have loved them as You have loved Me" (John 17:22,23, NKJV). Shared glory leads to Christian unity. Our unity, modeled after the divine example, lets the whole world know that God loves them.

21 "All these with one accord were devoting themselves to prayer . . ." (Acts 1:14, ESV). The apostles were "continually united in prayer" (CSB) before Pentecost.

"When the Day of Pentecost had fully come, they were all **22** together with one accord in one place" (Acts 2:1, NKJV). Christian unity is always a precursor to biblical evangelism. The result of Pentecost was a united, sharing, caring church (see Acts 2:44; 4:24, 32; 5:12).

> Christian unity is always a precursor to biblical evangelism.

23 "Just as each of us has one body with many members, and these members do not all have the same function, so in Christ we who are many form one body, and each member belongs to all the others" (Rom. 12:5, NIV). The analogy of the human body illustrates the importance of the spiritual body functioning in harmony.

"The man who eats everything must not look down on him **24** who does not, and the man who does not eat everything must not condemn the man who does, for God has accepted him" (Rom. 14:3, NIV). Matters of opinion should not be occasions for division because God has accepted both parties. It takes colossal gall to reject those whom God has received.

25 "So then let us pursue the things which make for peace and the building up of one another. Do not tear down the work of God

Scripture

for the sake of food . . ." (Rom. 14:19,20a, NASB). Following this admonition would end all food fights in the church between the Broccoli Brothers and the Ministers of Meat!

"Now may the God of endurance and encouragement grant you **26** agreement with one another, according to Jesus Christ, so that you may glorify the God and Father

> A united mind and voice will glorify God but a divided mind and voice will horrify Him.

of our Lord Jesus Christ with a united mind and voice" (Rom. 15:5,6, CSB). A united mind and voice will glorify God but a divided mind and voice will horrify Him.

27 "Accept one another, then, just as Christ accepted you, in order to bring praise to God" (Rom. 15:7, NIV). Were you perfect when Christ accepted you? Hardly. Then accept your imperfect brother or sister. This Christlike action will bring glory to God.

"I appeal to you, brothers, by the name of our Lord Jesus Christ, **28** that all of you agree and that there be no divisions among you, but that you be united in the same mind and the same judgment" (1 Cor. 1:10, ESV). But just how seriously have we taken this plea?

29 "Is not the cup of blessing which we bless a sharing in the blood of Christ? Is not the bread which we break a sharing in the body of Christ? Since there is one bread, we who are many are one body; for we all partake of the one bread" (1 Cor. 10:16,17, NASB). The Lord's Supper reminds us that we are one in Christ.

"For as the body is one and has many parts, and all the parts **30** of that body, though many, are one body—so also is Christ. For we were all baptized by one Spirit into one body—whether Jews or Greeks, whether slaves or free—and we were all made to drink of one Spirit" (1 Cor. 12:12,13, CSB). Through baptism, prompted by the Holy Spirit, we all come into the body of Christ the same way.

31 ". . . there should be no division in the body, but that the members should have the same care for one another. . . . Now you are Christ's body, and individually members of it" (1 Cor. 12:25,27,

NASB). Caring for each other will prevent "schism" (NKJV) in the body of Christ.

"And now I will show you the most excellent way. . . . And now **32** these three remain: faith, hope and love. But the greatest of these is love. Follow the way of love . . ." (1 Cor. 12:31b; 13:13,14a, NIV). Love is the pathway to unity and the preserver of unity.

> Love is the pathway to unity and the preserver of unity.

33 "For you are all sons of God through faith in Christ Jesus" (Gal. 3:26, NASB). A common faith in the Son of God brings us all into the family of God.

"For as many of you as have been baptized into Christ have put **34** on Christ" (Gal. 3:27, CSB). Faith *in* Christ will lead us to be baptized *into* Christ, where we then put *on* Christ.

35 "There is neither Jew nor Greek, there is neither slave nor free, there is neither male nor female, for you are all one in Christ Jesus" (Gal. 3:27,28, ESV). Here is the miracle of Christian unity! Our oneness in Christ transcends nationality, economic status, and gender.

"And he made known to us the mystery of his will according to **36** his good pleasure, which he purposed in Christ, to be put into effect when the times will have reached their fulfillment—to bring all things together under one head, even Christ" (Eph. 1:9,10, NIV). Unity in Christ has always been God's ultimate purpose.

37 "And God placed all things under his feet and appointed him to be head over everything for the church, which is his body, the fullness of him who fills everything in every way" (Eph. 1:22,23, NIV). When Christ is truly allowed to be the head of the church, harmony will be the result.

"For He Himself is our peace, who made both groups into one, **38** and broke down the barrier of the dividing wall" (Eph. 2:14, NASB). Christ is the great peacemaker and wall destroyer between Jews and Gentiles and other warring groups.

Scripture

39 "His purpose was to create in himself one new man out of the two, thus making peace, and in this one body to reconcile both of them to God through the cross, by which he put to death their hostility" (Eph. 2:15b,16, NIV). The death of Christ on the cross reconciled men to God—and to each other. The war is over!

"For through Him we both have access by one Spirit to the **40** Father" (Eph. 2:18, NKJV). All reconciled parties now have access to God through the Son of God and the Spirit of God.

41 "This mystery is that through the gospel the Gentiles are heirs together with Israel, members together of one body, and sharers together in the promise in Jesus Christ" (Eph. 3:6, NIV). Notice the "togetherness" Christ brings. We are heirs together, members together, sharers together.

> The family of God includes those already in heaven and those who are still upon earth.

"For this reason I kneel before the Father, from whom his whole family **42** in heaven and on earth derives its name" (Eph. 3:14,15, NIV). The family of God includes those already in heaven and those who are still upon earth.

43 "Make every effort to keep the unity of the Spirit through the bond of peace" (Eph. 4:3, NIV). Unity is not ours to manufacture. That is the work of the Holy Spirit. Our job is to maintain it through humility, gentleness, patience, forbearance, and love (Eph. 4:2).

"There is one body and one Spirit, just as also you were called **44** in one hope of your calling; one Lord, one faith, one baptism, one God and Father of all who is over all and through all and in all" (Eph. 4:4-6, NASB). Seven is the number for completeness and here is a unity of seven cardinal truths to be embraced by all. Omitting just one would break this powerful unity chain.

45 ". . . until we all attain to the unity of the faith, and of the knowledge of the Son of God, to a mature man, to the measure of the stature which belongs to the fulness of Christ" (Eph. 4:13,

NASB). The unity of the Spirit is a unity to maintain but here we find a unity to *attain*—the unity of the faith.

"From Him the whole body, fitted and knit together by every supporting ligament, promotes the growth of the body for building up itself in love by the proper working of each individual part" (Eph. 4:16, CSB). *Everyone* is vital to the effectual functioning of the body of Christ.

47 "Let all bitterness and wrath and anger and clamor and slander be put away from you, along with all malice. Be kind to one another, tenderhearted, forgiving one another, as God in Christ forgave you" (Eph. 4:31,32, ESV). Nothing will restore unity quicker than a sincere application of this admonition.

"Whatever happens, conduct yourselves in a manner worthy of the gospel of Christ. Then, whether I come and see you or only hear about you in my absence, I will know that you stand firm in one spirit, contending as one man for the faith of the gospel" (Phil. 1:27, NIV). Here is the conduct that will honor Christ and advance His cause!

49 "If you have any encouragement from being united with Christ, if any comfort from his love, if any fellowship with the Spirit, if any tenderness and compassion, then make my joy complete by being like-minded, having the same love, being one in spirit and purpose" (Phil. 2:1,2, NIV). Christian unity should bring joy to all Christians!

"Do nothing out of selfish ambition or vain conceit, but in humility consider others better than yourselves. Each one of you should look not only to your own interests, but also to the interests of others" (Phil. 2:3,4, NIV). Following this advice would bring an end to nearly every problem in the church.

51 "I plead with Euodia and I plead with Syntyche to agree with each other in the Lord" (Phil. 4:2, NIV). How do we learn to agree with each other? "In the Lord!"

"For I want you to know what a great conflict I have for you and for those in Laodicea . . . that their hearts may be encouraged, being knit together in love . . ." (Col. 2:1,2a, NKJV). Paul had a great concern that all believers would be "united in love" (NIV).

53 "Therefore, as God's chosen people, holy and dearly loved, clothe yourselves with compassion, kindness, humility, gentleness and patience. Bear with each other and forgive whatever grievances you may have against one another. Forgive as the Lord forgave you. And over all these virtues put on love, which binds them all together in perfect unity. Let the peace of Christ rule in your hearts, since as members of one body you were called to peace. And be thankful" (Col. 3:12-14, NIV).

"About brotherly love: you don't need me to write you because **54** you yourselves are taught by God to love one another. In fact, you are doing this toward all the brothers in the entire region of Macedonia. But we encourage you to do so even more" (1 Thess. 4:9,10, CSB). If Paul didn't need to write to them about love, I don't need to comment here!

55 "Let brotherly love continue" (Heb. 13:1, CSB). Love is a continuous action.

"If you really fulfill the royal law according to the Scripture, **56** 'You shall love your neighbor as yourself,' you are doing well. But if you show partiality, you are committing sin and are convicted by the law as transgressors" (Jas. 2:8,9, ESV). This is the law of our Royal Sovereign. How dare we disobey!

57 "Above all, keep fervent in your love for one another, because love covers a multitude of sins" (1 Pet. 4:8, NASB). Trajan, a Roman emperor, wrote in admiration of Christians, "Behold, how they love one another!"

"We proclaim to you what we have seen and heard, so that you **58** also may have fellowship with us. And our fellowship is with the Father and with his Son, Jesus Christ" (1 John 1:3, NIV). There are two kinds of fellowship: horizontal (fellowship with believers) and vertical (fellowship with God and Christ).

59 "He who says he is in the light, and hates his brother, is in darkness until now. He who loves his brother abides in the light, and there is no cause for stumbling in him. But he who hates his brother is in darkness and walks in darkness, and does not know where he is going, because the darkness has blinded his eyes" (1 John 1:9-11, NKJV). Love is the light that banishes the darkness.

"For this is the message you have heard from the beginning, that we should love one another" (1 John 3:11, ESV). Love has **60** never ceased to be in force.

61 "We know that we have passed from death to life, because we love our brothers. Anyone who does not love remains in death. Anyone who hates his brother is a murderer, and you know that no murderer has eternal life in him" (1 John 3:14,15, NIV). Love of the brethren proves that we have made this sacred passing over.

"This is how we know what love is: Jesus Christ laid down his **62** life for us. And we ought to lay down our lives for our brothers" (1 John 3:16, NIV). But we will not be able to do that until we first learn how to lay down a few differences we may have.

63 "And this is His commandment: that we should believe on the name of His Son Jesus Christ and love one another, as He gave us commandment" (1 John 3:23, NKJV). Faith in Christ should be accompanied by love for our Christian brethren.

"Dear friends, let us love one another, for love comes from **64** God. Everyone who loves has been born of God and knows God. Whoever does not love does not know God, because God is love. This is how God showed his love among us: He sent his one and only Son into the world that we might live through him. This is love: not that we loved God, but that he loved us and sent his Son as an atoning sacrifice for our sins. Dear friends, since God so loved us, we also ought to love one another" (1 John 4:7-11, NIV).

65 "If anyone says, 'I love God,' and hates his brother, he is a liar; for he who does not love his brother whom he has seen cannot love God whom he has not seen. And this commandment we have

> **Love is not optional—
> it is obligatory!**

from him: whoever loves God must also love his brother" (1 John 4:20,21, ESV). Love is not optional—it is obligatory!

"And after this I looked, and behold, a great multitude that no one could number, from every nation, from all tribes and peoples and languages, standing before the throne and before the Lamb, clothed in white robes, with palm branches in their hands, and crying out with a loud voice, 'Salvation belongs to our God who sits on the throne, and to the Lamb!'" (Rev. 7:9,10, ESV). It doesn't get any better than this! "When we all get to heaven, what a day of rejoicing that will be!"

God has spoken.
The Scripture cannot be broken.
It's more than just a token.
May the circle be unbroken—together in Christ!

Bible Version Abbreviations

CSB (Christian Standard Bible)
ESV (English Standard Version)
NASB (New American Standard Bible)
NIV (New International Version)
NKJV (New King James Version)

Chapter Two

TURNING OUR DREAMS INTO PRAYERS
PRAYERS FOR UNITY

Charles Spurgeon said, "All the Christian virtues are locked up in the word prayer." Prayer has been called the key of the morning and the bolt at night. "More things are wrought (accomplished) by prayer than this world dreams of," observed Alfred Lord Tennyson. If we would only turn our dreams into prayers, what great things might happen?

The Westminster Confession defines prayer as "an offering up of our desires unto God for things agreeable to His will, in the name of Christ, with confession of our sins and thankful acknowledgement of His mercies." Scripture places a high premium on prayer. It is one of the most spiritual things we can do. Praying for Christian unity is an extreme spiritual activity.

> Praying for Christian unity is an extreme spiritual activity.

Jesus Christ is the finest example of prayer. Although He was the Son of God, He still spent a great amount of time in prayer. In the predawn hours, He prayed. "Very early in the morning, while it was still dark, Jesus got up, left the house and went off to a solitary place, where he prayed" (Mark 1:35). Sometimes he prayed all night long. "Jesus went out to a mountainside to pray, and spent the night praying to God" (Luke 6:12).

THE MODEL PRAYER

No wonder the disciples asked Jesus, the most spiritual man who ever lived, to teach them to pray! In what is sometimes called "The Lord's Prayer," although it might be more aptly called "The Model Prayer," Jesus taught his disciples how to pray (Matt. 6:9-13). He said, "Pray, then, in this way:

Our Father in heaven,
Hallowed be Your name.
Your kingdom come.
Your will be done
On earth as it is in heaven.
Give us this day our daily bread.
And forgive us our debts,
As we forgive our debtors.
And do not lead us into temptation,
But deliver us from the evil one.
For Yours is the kingdom,
and the power and the glory,
forever. Amen.

At the heart of this prayer is the heart of the message of unity—forgiveness. We hallow the name of the Father, we hasten the expansion of the kingdom and we hearken to the will of God when we forgive men their transgressions. Jesus declared, "But if you do not forgive men, then your Father will not forgive your transgressions" (Matt. 6:15, NASB). An unforgiving heart is a terrible barrier to Christian unity. As disciples of our Lord, let us pray this prayer together in Christ:

> An unforgiving heart is a terrible barrier to Christian unity.

reverently,
thoughtfully,
and purposefully.

THE PRAYER OF A KING

Jesus prayed for Christian unity. The longest recorded prayer of Jesus is found in John 17, which has been called the "Holy of Holies" of the New Testament. Martin Luther said this text should have been written in letters of gold. Why? Because it is the prayer of a king. But not just any king, mind you. The Bible describes him as "KING OF KINGS AND LORD OF LORDS" (Rev. 19:16).

There is not a scene more amazing than a king on his knees in prayer. George Washington knelt in the snow at Valley Forge and asked God for divine guidance. Abraham Lincoln, during the dark days of the Civil War, said, "I have been driven many times to my knees by the overwhelming conviction that I had no where else to go. My own wisdom, and that of all about me, seemed insufficient for the day."

Still, Christ, the praying king, is a dying king. This prayer is offered to God just a scant twelve hours from the cross. How would you pray if you knew you had only twelve hours to live? For what would you pray? More properly stated, for whom would you pray?

> How would you pray if you knew you had only twelve hours to live?

JESUS PRAYS FOR HIMSELF

Of all the things that Jesus could have prayed for, Christian unity was at the heart of his prayer (John 17:11,20-23). Let us reverently enter the "Holy of Holies" and give audience to the High Priestly prayer of Jesus. First, Jesus prays for himself that He might be glorified. Shhh. Listen.

> **Father, the hour has come. Glorify Your Son, that Your Son also may glorify You, as You have given Him authority over all flesh, that He should give eternal life to as many as You have given Him. And this is eternal life, that they may know You, the only true God, and Jesus Christ, whom You have sent. I have glorified You on the earth. I have finished the work which You have given Me to do. And now, O Father, glorify Me together with Yourself, with the glory which I had with You before the world was (John 17:1-5).**

"Glory" is the key word in this first petition. Why does Jesus request to be glorified with the glory He had with God before the creation of the world? Because glory is God's appointed means to unity. Biblical authors always used "glory" to describe "character." To talk about God's glory was to talk about His character. We see God's glory, or character, displayed in the perfectly unified persons of the trinity. "And the glory which You gave Me I have given them, that they may be one just as We are one" (v. 22).

Jesus Prays for His Disciples

Next, Jesus prays for His disciples. He prays that they might be sanctified. This is the longest portion of the prayer, but unity is still at the heart of this second petition (John 17:11).

I have manifested Your name to the men whom You have given Me out of the world. They were Yours, You gave them to Me, and they have kept Your word. Now they have known that all things which You have given Me are from You. For I have given to them the words which You have given Me; and they have received them, and have known surely that I came forth from You; and they have believed that You sent Me.

I pray for them. I do not pray for the world but for those whom You have given Me, for they are Yours. And all Mine are Yours, and Yours are Mine, and I am glorified in them. Now I am no longer in the world, and I come to You. Holy Father, keep through Your name those whom You have given Me, that they may be one as We are. While I was with them in the world, I kept them in Your name. Those whom You gave Me I have kept; and none of them is lost except the son of perdition, that the Scripture might be fulfilled. But now I come to You, and these things I speak in the world, that they may have My joy fulfilled in themselves. I have given them Your word; and the world has hated them because they are not of the world, just as I am not of the world. I do not pray that You should take them out of the world, but that You should keep them from the evil one. They are not of the world, just as I am not of the world. Sanctify them by Your truth. Your word is truth. As You sent Me into the world, I also have sent them into the world. And for their sakes I sanctify Myself, that they also may be sanctified by the truth (John 17:6-19).

This petition asks for the protection of the disciples for the purpose of Christian unity: "Holy Father, protect them by the power of your name—the name you gave me—so that they may be one as we are one" (v. 11, NIV). The Father and Son are one. This is the divine model for Christian unity. The Father and Son are one in name, one in nature, one in enjoyment, one in purpose. Brothers and sisters, together in Christ, children of the same Father, are one in name (Christian), one in nature (partakers of the divine nature), one in enjoyment (the Spirit-led Christian life), and one in purpose (preparing themselves and others for eternity in heaven).

Jesus Prays for All Believers

There is a powerful shift in emphasis as Jesus begins the third and final petition of this wonderful prayer. It is as though His eyes, which had been looking up to heaven (v. 1), are now directed to a far and distant horizon. Through the long tunnel of time, believers in the future come into His vision and into His prayer. This is the night Jesus prayed for you and me. There is a holy hush, a pregnant pause, and then the sacred supplication continues.

I do not pray for these alone, but also for those who will believe in Me through their word; that they all may be one, as You, Father, are in Me, and I in You; that they also may be one in Us, that the world may believe that You sent Me. And the glory which You gave Me I have given them, that they may be one just as We are one: I in them, and You in Me; that they may be made perfect in one, and that the world may know that You have sent Me, and have loved them as You have loved Me.

Father, I desire that they also whom You gave Me may be with Me where I am, that they may behold My glory which You have given Me; for You loved Me before the foundation of the world. O righteous Father! The world has not known You, but I have known You; and these have known that You sent Me. And I have declared to them Your name, and will declare it, that the love with which You loved Me may be in them, and I in them (John 7:20-26).

The unity Jesus envisioned is:
- Christ-centered. "I . . . pray . . . for those who will believe in Me."
- Bible-based. "I . . . pray . . . for those who will believe in Me through their word."
- People-predominant. "I . . . pray . . . for those who will believe in Me through their word; that they all may be one . . . that the world may believe . . ."

One day I was reading this prayer, and in the translation I was using, a certain word seemed to keep leaping off the page. Seventeen times in John 17 the word "world" appears! This should not surprise us. The Golden Verse of the Bible says, "For God so loved the world. . . ." Jesus prayed for the oneness of all believers so "that the world may believe . . . that the world may know . . . that they . . . may be with Me."

| Christian unity is absolutely essential to world evangelism. |

Christian unity is absolutely essential to world evangelism.

Paul's Prayer for the Ephesians

If there is any book in the New Testament that emphasizes Christian unity, it would be Paul's letter to the body of Christ in Ephesus. Again and again the point is made that our unity is "in Christ," a phrase that is repeated many times. Chapter 4:1-6, in particular, addresses the attitudes that lead to unity (humility, gentleness, patience, forbearance, and love) and the seven articles of unity—

- One body
- One Spirit
- One hope
- One Lord
- One faith
- One baptism
- One God and Father of all—over all, through all, in all

Two kinds of unity are mentioned in Chapter 4. There is a unity to maintain, and that is the unity of the Holy Spirit. "Make every effort to keep the unity of the Spirit through the bond of peace" (v. 3). Our unity is a gift of the Spirit that is to be maintained, not manufactured. The second kind of unity mentioned in this chapter is that which we are to strive to attain—unity in the faith and knowledge of Christ. "Until we all reach unity in the faith and in the knowledge of the Son of God and become mature, attaining to the whole measure of the fullness of Christ" (v. 13).

What is sometimes overlooked is Paul's prayer for the Ephesians that precedes his teaching on unity in the body of Christ (Ephesians 3:14-21, NIV). Fervent prayer is a precursor to effective unity. Paul is far away in Rome, in prison, but still he prays. Let's join him in spirit as the great apostle kneels in prayer to pray for the whole family of God.

> For this reason I kneel before the Father,
> from whom his whole family in heaven
> and on earth derives its name.
> I pray that out of his glorious riches he may
> strengthen you with power through his Spirit
> in your inner being,
> so that Christ may dwell in your hearts
> through faith.
> And I pray that you, being rooted
> and established in love,
> may have power, together with all the saints,
> to grasp how wide and long and high
> and deep is the love of Christ,
> and to know this love that surpasses knowledge—
> that you may be filled to the measure
> of all the fullness of God.

Now to him who is able
to do immeasurably more than all
we ask or imagine,
according to his power that is at work within us,
to him be glory in the church
and in Christ Jesus
throughout all generations,
for ever and ever!
Amen.

Surely what Paul prayed for believers in Ephesus to have are requisites for unity of all Christians everywhere—being empowered by the Holy Spirit, enjoying the indwelling presence of Christ, knowing a love that surpasses knowledge—this is the sort of stuff that will strengthen our unity "in Christ."

PRAYERS OF THE CHURCH FATHERS

Prayers of church leaders in the postapostolic era often included petitions for understanding of Scripture, unity of spirit, and the restoration of the church. Three prayers representative of this time are found in *The Macmillian Book of Earliest Christian Prayers* © 1988 by F. Forrester Church and Terrence J. Mulry (Collier Books).

Let us ask the Lord to broaden our ideas, make them clearer, and bring them nearer to the truth, that we may understand the other things too that he has revealed to his prophets. May we study the Holy Spirit's writings under the guidance of the Spirit himself and compare one spiritual interpretation with another, so that our explanation of the texts may be worthy of God and the Holy Spirit, who inspired them. May we do this through Christ Jesus, our Lord, to whom glory and power belong and will belong though all the ages. Amen.

Origen of Alexandria

O God the Father:
Origin of divinity,
Good beyond all that is good,
Fair beyond all that is fair,
In whom is calmness, peace, concord:

Do thou make up
The dissensions which divide us
From each other,
And bring us back
Into the unity of love,
Which to thy divine nature
May bear some likeness.

As thou art above all things,
Make us one by the unanimity
Of a good mind,
That through the embrace of charity,
And the bonds of godly affection
We spiritually may be one,
As well in ourselves
As in each other,
By that peace of thine
Which maketh all things peaceful:

Through the grace,
The mercy, and the tenderness
Of thine only begotten Son,
Jesus, the Christ, our Lord.

Dionysius of Alexandria

Let us pray to the Lord alone without ceasing to ask and, with faith in receiving, straightforward and of one mind, entreating both groaning and weeping, as those who are placed between the ruins of the moaning and the remains of the fearful, between the manifold destruction of the fallen and the paltry strength of the standing, ought to pray. Let us ask for peace to be restored sooner, to be succored quickly in our hiding places and dangers, for what the Lord deigns to manifest to his servants to be fulfilled: the restoration of his Church, the security of our salvation, serenity after the rains, light after darkness, peaceful calm after storms and dangers, blessed aids of his fatherly love, the accustomed grandeurs of his divine majesty, by which the blasphemy of the persecutors may be beaten back, and the penance of the lapsed may be accomplished, and the strong and stable faith of the persevering may glory.

Cyprian of Carthage

The Peace Prayer

A prayer that has been attributed to Francis of Assisi (1181–1226), founder of the Franciscans, was probably written by someone else. "The Peace Prayer" first appeared in France in 1912 as an anonymous piece in a small magazine called *La Clochette* ("The Little Bell"). The first translation in English that we know of was in 1936 when Kirby Page, a Disciples of Christ minister, published it in his book *Living Courageously.* Regardless of its authorship, it emphasizes man's longing to be used of God to be a peacemaker.

> Where there is discord, let me bring union. / Where there is doubt, let me bring faith.

Lord, make me an instrument of Your peace.
Where there is hatred, let me bring love.
Where there is injury, let me bring pardon.
Where there is discord, let me bring union.
Where there is doubt, let me bring faith.
Where there is error, let me bring truth.
Where there is despair, let me bring hope.
Where there is sadness, let me bring joy.

Where there is darkness, let me bring light.

O Divine Master,
grant that I may not so much seek
to be consoled as to console,
to be understood as to understand,
to be loved as to love.

For it is in giving that we receive.
It is in pardoning that we are pardoned.
It is in dying that we are born to eternal life.

A Prayer for Unity

The following prayer, entitled simply "A Prayer for Unity," appears at the conclusion of James DeForest Murch's monumental work *Christians Only, A History of the Restoration Movement* (Standard Publishing, 1962). I have taken the liberty of changing "Thee" and "Thou" to "You" and "Your" and reformatting the lines into stylistic format with no words other than those mentioned removed or altered.

> We long for the visible realization of the unity for which Christ prayed.

Gracious God, our heavenly Father,
we thank You for the church of Jesus Christ.
We thank You that You did so love us
as to send Your only begotten Son into the world
to give His life a ransom for all men
who believe in His name.

We thank You, our God,
that we have been purchased
by His precious atoning blood,
born again and made a part of His glorious body
the church.
We thank You for the blessed fellowship we know in You
through Your dear Son—

one flock, one fold, and one Shepherd.
We find in Jesus Christ our life, our hope, our all.

We thank You for Your Holy Word and the Holy Spirit
whereby we are grounded, upheld and guided,
and preserved in holy communion with You.

As we look upon the outward divisions of the church
in the world our hearts are pained.
God, forgive our humanisms, our perversions,
and our feverish ways which promote divisions,
which keep us from fellowship one with another
and which hinder
the evangelization of the world.
We long for the visible realization
of the unity for which Christ prayed.
We would surrender our wills completely to You
that Your will may be done in us
to the unity of Your people
and to Your everlasting glory.

We pray Your divine blessing
upon all those movements and agencies
which seek in sincerity
the true and ultimate unity of Your people in the earth.
Guide them in Your truth to do Your will.
Bless especially, we beseech You,
those earnest souls who have dedicated their lives
to the achievement of this holy purpose.
Keep them in Your will and way.
Deliver them from presumptuous thoughts,
precipitous acts,
and shameful compromises.

Hinder and destroy, we beseech You,
every device of men or of Satan
which would mar the pattern of the church
which Jesus built

and which His chosen apostles have revealed to us
in Your Holy Word.

Forbid, O God,
that unity which would compromise Your eternal truth,
condone evil,
dampen our zeal for lost souls,
consent to barren profession,
bear no spiritual fruit,
take pride in outward show,
seek political power,
and number in its company
a people who praise You with their lips
but whose hearts are far from You.
Fulfill the heartening promise of our Lord
that the gates of hell shall not prevail
against Your church.

Help us to know the mind of Christ
and His will for us in all things pertaining to His church,
that in His greatness we may rise above our littleness,
in His strength we shall lose our weaknesses,
in His peace we may bury all discord;
that in His truth and righteousness
we may march—
the united church militant
accomplishing the work You have set for us
in our day and time.

At last, we pray,
enfold us in the one church triumphant,
the family of God,
to dwell with You forever.
And unto You
we will ascribe all honor and glory
through Jesus Christ, our Lord.
Amen.

A Prayer for Unity in the Church of Christ

Don Reece compiled a unique prayer for unity that appeared in the Winter 1991 issue of *One Body*.

> O Christ, too long Thy Holy Church has been
> Divided; torn and rent with rancorous strife
> O'er trivial things; too long has failed to hear
> The dying prayer, of Thee, who gave Thy life
> The Church to purchase; somehow failed to see
> That it is Thine; that to it all the ones
> Whom Thou dost save are added; and that we
> Are brothers each to each who are God's sons.
>
> Help us, O Christ, who talk of unity;
> Who proudly say we have no creed but Thee,
> To see our creeds, unwritten—our deep loss!—
> To shake them off, and in Thy liberty
> Stand fast, as, once again, united, we
> Call men to rally 'round Thy holy cross.

A Prayer for Unity

Rubel Shelly, author of *I Just Want to Be a Christian* and *The Jesus Proposal*, has written this untitled prayer.

> Holy God, making Yourself known to us as our Loving Father, revealed to us most perfectly in our Lord Jesus Christ, and ever-present with us by Your Holy Spirit, we pray to be one as You are One.
>
> Blessed God, we marvel at the sheer mystery of Your nature—Three as One, distinct in person but One Godhead over all, holy individuals
>
> > Who are nevertheless Whole in Community.
> >
> > Thank You, Dear God, for calling us out of broken, isolated selfhood to participation in Your wholeness and unity;

Teach us, Loving God, to respect one another in personality and gifts and imperfect understandings of Your perfect will.

Enfold us, O God, in One Holy Community with You and one another—bound together not by wisdom or power but by Your lovingkindness.

God our Father, let us be Your indivisible Family.

Your daughters, O Father, who bear both holiness and grace;

Your sons, O Father, who exhibit Your creativity and strength;

Your children, O Father, always one in spite of our childish quarreling.

God the Son, love us gently as Your Bride.

Evoke beauty, O Lord, where sin has left us ugly and scarred;

Robe with radiant holiness, O Master, that we know is Your pure grace;

Empower fidelity, O Lover of our souls, for we are inclined to infidelity.

God the Holy Spirit, indwell us as Your Holy Temple.

As building stones, set us on the one sure foundation;

As living stones, make us vibrant with Your life within;

As unworthy stones, build us into a holy sanctuary on the Chief Foundation Stone the workmen rejected.

Triune God Who has lived in perfect community from eternity past, forgive us for our failure to receive the gift of community, harmony, and oneness You have offered. Renew us that we may be able to accept the unity our ego and pride have resisted. And so let us bear witness yet to a world that watches in its strife and divisions how good and pleasant it is when Your people dwell together as one church.

Amen.

> Let us bear witness yet to a world that watches in its strife and divisions how good and pleasant it is when Your people dwell together as one church.

A Lament over the Body of Christ

Rob McCray fashioned a haunting and poignant "lament" that appeared in the Spring 1996 *One Body*.

Jesus Is Weeping

Jesus is weeping—
with the pain of His body
torn in many pieces.
As each bleeding part of His body
claims to be the healthy whole,
Jesus is weeping.

Jesus is weeping—
because His beloved children
find it so difficult to simply
trust in His grace.
He offers a free gift;
but as His children argue
over who can receive His gift,
Jesus is weeping.

Jesus is weeping—
for His unanswered prayer
the night He was betrayed,
that all who believed in Him
would be one,

and the world would know
that He was from the Father.
Knowing that His followers
have betrayed Him,
Jesus is weeping.

Jesus is weeping—
for all the lost souls
who will never hear the gospel
of His grace.
Because those who would preach it
are too absorbed with arguing
over who is saved.
And as His disciples
fervently defend their disunity,
Jesus is weeping.

And so should we all.
It is the Sabbath
and I would go and anoint the body . . .
but it is buried in too many tombs.

Dear Lord and Father of Mankind

John Greenleaf Whittier (1807–1892) was a Quaker poet who in his time was surpassed in popularity only by Longfellow. In 1872 he wrote a poem that was later set to music by Frederick C. Maker in 1887. It was written in response to some of the absurd and even divisive things he had observed in some religious circles. It speaks to our longing for peace and tranquility in these days of foolish strivings.

> Dear Lord and Father of mankind,
> Forgive our foolish ways!

Dear Lord and Father of mankind,
Forgive our foolish ways!
Reclothe us in our rightful mind;
In purer lives Thy service find,
In deeper rev'rence, praise.

In simple trust like theirs who heard,
Beside the Syrian Sea,
The gracious calling of the Lord,
Let us, like them, without a word,
Rise up and follow Thee.

Drop Thy still dews of quietness,
Till all our strivings cease;
Take from our souls the strain and stress,
And let our ordered lives confess
The beauty of Thy peace.

Breathe through the heats of our desire
Thy coolness and Thy balm;
Let sense be dumb, let flesh retire;
Speak through the earthquake, wind, and fire,
O still small voice of calm!

Another prayer seeking forgiveness for hurtful words spoken or
thoughtless deeds done is a poem by C.M. Battersby, set to music by
Charles H. Gabriel. Augustine said that when one sings he prays
twice. Singing is sometimes a special form of prayer. Battersby's
poem/prayer/hymn is simply called . . .

An Evening Prayer

If I have wounded any soul today,
If I have caused one foot to go astray,
If I have walked in my own willful way,
Dear Lord, forgive!

If I have uttered idle words or vain,
If I have turned aside from want or pain,
Lest I myself shall suffer through the strain,
Dear Lord, forgive!

If I have been perverse or hard or cold,
If I have longed for shelter in Thy fold,
When Thou hast given me some fort to hold,
Dear Lord, forgive!

Forgive the sins I have confessed to Thee;
Forgive the secret sins I do not see;
O guide me, love me, and my keeper be,
Dear Lord, Amen.

The Apostolic Benediction

In what is often called "The Apostolic Benediction," Paul closes his second letter to the church in Corinth with a prayer that invokes the unity of the Godhead (2 Cor. 13:14, NIV). The Father, Son, and Holy Spirit are one—one as we are one when they are with us.

**"May the grace of our Lord Jesus Christ,
and the love of God,
and the fellowship of the Holy Spirit
be with you all."**

Amen, Father. We are one in Your love.
Amen, Son. We are one by Your grace.
Amen, Holy Spirit. We are one in Your fellowship.

Chapter Three

O FOR A THOUSAND CHRISTIANS TO SING!

SONGS OF UNITY

Come, Christians, join to sing. Alleluia! Amen!
Loud praise to Christ our King; Alleluia! Amen!
Let all, with heart and voice, Before His throne rejoice;
Praise is His gracious choice: Alleluia! Amen!

Christian H. Bateman

There is nothing that demonstrates our unity and pleases God more than when Christians join their voices in songs of praise to Him. It is one thing for a Christian to sing. How much more glorious is it, as Charles Wesley penned, when a thousand Christians unite to sing their great Redeemer's praise!

A spirit of unity promotes praise. The apostle Paul wished this for the church in Rome. "May the God who gives endurance and encouragement give you a spirit of unity among yourselves as you follow Jesus Christ, so that with one heart and mouth you may glorify the God and Father of our Lord Jesus Christ" (Rom. 15:5,6, NIV). A spirit of unity will promote songs of unity. And there are many songs of unity that God has led select men and women to compose and millions more to sing.

> "So that with one heart and mouth you may glorify the God and Father of our Lord Jesus Christ."

The creation of the universe began with singing, the morning stars singing together and the sons of God shouting for joy (Job 38:7). The nation of Israel had their own Psalter, the Psalms (lit., "Book of Praises"). Psalm 100 says, "Come before His presence with singing . . . Enter into His gates with thanksgiving, and into His courts with praise . . . " (Psalm 100:2,4). Singing was always an expression of unity.

45

The Songs of Ascent (Psalms 120–134), a collection of special songs the Jewish people would sing as they ascended the hills to Jerusalem for one of the Jewish festivals, includes one that is a beautiful song depicting unity: Psalm 133:1-3. Jesus Himself probably sang this song with His parents as they ascended the hills to Jerusalem. "And His parents used to go to Jerusalem every year at the Feast of the Passover. And when He became twelve, they went up there according to the custom of the Feast" (Luke 2:41,42, NASB). This Davidic Song of Ascent may have been on His mind the night He prayed for unity (John 17:20-23).

> How good and pleasant it is
>   When brothers live together in unity!
> It is like precious oil poured on the head,
>   running down on the beard,
> running down on Aaron's beard,
>   down upon the collar of his robes.
> It is as if the dew of Hermon
>   Were falling on Mount Zion.
> For there the Lord bestows his blessing,
>   even life forevermore.

The return of the Prodigal Son was celebrated with singing (Luke 16:25). The Last Supper concluded with Jesus and the disciples singing a hymn before they went to the Mount of Olives (Matt. 26:30). (That hymn included Psalm 118, the last psalm in what was called "The Great Hallel," Psalms 113–118. It was customary to sing the Hallel at the Jewish Passover.) Paul and Silas sang hymns to God while they were in prison in Philippi (Acts 16:25). The Christians in Corinth were told to sing with both the spirit and the understanding (1 Cor. 14:15). In Ephesians 5:19 and Colossians 3:16 Paul instructed believers to sing a variety of songs—"psalms, hymns and spiritual songs." The letter to the Hebrews mentions singing praises in the midst of the congregation (2:12) as well as continual praise (13:15). Those who were happy were told to express their joy in singing (Jas. 5:13). The Revelation of Jesus Christ contains several references to joyful singing and triumphant praise that takes place in heaven (5:9-14; 7:9-12; 15:2-4).

One of the earliest hymns of the church may be found in Paul's letter to Timothy. Many Bible scholars and commentators believe it was sung like a "chant." If we had to give it a title, it would seem to be appropriate to call it simply what Paul does in 1 Timothy 3:16 (ESV), "The Mystery of Godliness." In six compact "verses," the song exalts Jesus Christ—His incarnation, vindication, visualization, proclamation, reception, and ascension. It is a song that describes what the early Christians believed about their Savior.

He was manifested in the flesh,
vindicated by the Spirit,
seen by angels,
proclaimed among the nations,
believed on in the world,
taken up to glory.

Classic Hymns

We hear much today, too much perhaps, about how music divides churches. Yet I have often been impressed with how the hymns of the church have united us. When we sing a song, we do not usually even think about who wrote the song, what church or denomination that person represented, or what doctrinal beliefs he or she may have held. Even though a hymn writer may not have come from our religious background, we heartily sing his or her hymn and feel one with all those joining their voices with us. Many of the hymn writers have expressed a desire for togetherness in Christ in their songs.

> I have often been impressed with how the hymns of the church have united us.

Here are a few examples of unity-minded songs that are in the public domain (or whose authors have given us permission to quote them).

The Church's One Foundation
Samuel J. Stone (1839–1900)

The church's one foundation
Is Jesus Christ her Lord;
She is His new creation,

By water and the Word:
From heav'n He came and sought her
To be His holy bride,
With His own blood He bought her,
And for her life He died.

Elect from every nation,
Yet one o'er all the earth,
Her charter of salvation,
One Lord, one faith, one birth;
One holy name she blesses,
Partakes one holy food,
And to one hope she presses,
With every grace endued.

'Mid toil and tribulation,
And tumult of her war,
She waits the consummation
Of peace forevermore;
Till with the vision glorious,
Her longing eyes are blest,
And the great church victorious
Shall be the church at rest.

Note the seven uses of "one" in the second stanza, including "One Lord, one faith, one birth." Stone must have equated the "one birth" with the "one baptism" of Ephesians 4:4, "one Lord, one faith, one baptism." The use of "by water and the word" in the first stanza is reflective of Paul's teaching in Ephesians 5:25.

Elect from every nation,
Yet one o'er all the earth.

In Christ There Is No East or West
John Oxenham (1852–1941)

In Christ there is no East or West,
In Him no South or North;
But one great fellowship of love
Throughout the whole wide earth.

In Him shall true hearts everywhere
Their high communion find;
His service is the golden cord
Close binding all mankind.

Join hands then, brothers of the faith,
Whate'er your race may be;
Who serves my Father as a son
Is surely kin to me.

In Christ now meet both East and West;
In Him meet South and North.
All Christly souls are one in Him
Throughout the whole wide earth.

There are no national boundaries that contain true Christianity. Notice that the phrase "in Christ" or "in Him" appears six times in the great hymn. Truly our unity is to be found only "in Christ." All those who

> All Christly souls are one in Him
> Throughout the whole wide earth.

are sons and daughters of the Father are brothers and sisters "in Him."

HOW SWEET, HOW HEAVENLY
Joseph Swain (1761–1796)

How sweet, how heav'nly, is the sight,
When those that love the Lord
In one another's peace delight,
And so fulfill the Word.

When each can feel his brother's sigh,
And with him bear a part;
When sorrow flows from eye to eye,
And joy from heart to heart.

When, free from envy, scorn and pride,
Our wishes all above,
Each can his brother's failings hide,
And shows a brother's love.

Songs

When love in one delightful stream
Through every bosom flows;
When union sweet and dear esteem
In every action glows.

Love is the golden chain that binds
The happy souls above;
And he's an heir of heav'n who finds
His bosom glow with love.

This hymn, written in 1792, four years before Swain's death, speaks in glowing terms of brotherly love. In fact, love is mentioned

> Love is the golden chain that binds
> The happy souls above.

five times in this short text. Those who "love the Lord" will also "feel their brother's sigh" (how good are we at doing that?) and hide their brother's sins (it is more tempting to expose them). Love covers a multitude of sins (Jas. 5:20).

LOVE ONE ANOTHER

Angry words! O let them never
From my tongue unbridled slip;
May the heart's best impulse ever
Check them ere they soil the lip.

Love is much too pure and holy,
Friendship is too sacred far,
For a moment's reckless folly
Thus to desolate and mar.

Let our words be sweetly spoken
Let kind thoughts be greatly stirred;
Show our love to one another
With abundance of kind words.

Refrain
"Love one another," thus saith the Savior;
Children, obey the Father's blest command.

"Love one another," thus saith the Savior;
'Tis the Father's blest command.

This song, attributed simply to a Sunday School teacher in 1867 (with Betty Bender adding the third verse in 1992), underscores the importance of speaking with kindness to (and about) one another. Many a friendship, marriage, and church has been split asunder by "angry words." "Be kind and compassionate to one another, forgiving each other, just as in Christ God forgave you" (Eph. 4:32).

BRETHREN, WE HAVE MET TO WORSHIP
George Atkins (19th Century)

Brethren, we have met to worship
And adore the Lord our God;
Will you pray with all your power,
While we try to preach the Word?
All in vain unless the Spirit
Of the Holy One comes down;
Brethren, pray, and holy manna
Will be showered all around.

Let us love our God supremely,
Let us love each other too;
Let us love and pray for sinners
Till our God makes all things new.
Then He'll call us home to heaven,
At His table we'll sit down;
Christ will gird Himself and serve us
With sweet manna all around.

Written in 1819, this hymn draws a contrast between meeting to worship here and assembling for worship in heaven. Love for God (adoration), love for each other (unity), and love for sinners (evangelism) is the triple theme. If we don't love each other, we can't say we love God. If we don't love each other, it's unlikely that we will love sinners.

Come, Risen Lord!
G.W. Briggs (1875–1959)

Come, risen Lord, and deign to be our guest;
Nay, let us be Thy guests; the feast is Thine;
Thyself at Thine own board make manifest,
In Thine own sacrament of bread and wine.

We meet, as in that upper room they met;
Thou at the table, blessing, yet dost stand;
"This is my body" so Thou givest yet:
Faith still receives the cup as from Thy hand.

One body we, one body who partake,
One Church united in communion blest;
One Name we bear, one bread of life we break,
With all Thy saints on earth and saints at rest.

One with each other, Lord, for one in Thee,
Who art one Savior and one living Head;
Then open Thou our eyes, that we may see;
Be known to us in breaking of the bread.

I came across this hymn during my visit to the Berlin Street Church in Belfast, Northern Ireland. It is taken from *The Christian Hymnary* (1938), a hymnal published in Great Britain on behalf of Churches of Christ. Surely in the Lord's Supper we are "one church united in communion blest." May the living Christ open our eyes to that truth the next time we break the bread and drink the cup.

> One body we, one body who partake, / One Church united in communion blest.

How Blest and How Joyous (Unity Song)
M.C. Kurfrees (1856–1931)

How blest and how joyous will be the glad day,
When heart beats to heart in the work of the Lord;
When Christians united shall swell the grand lay,
Divisions all ended, triumphant His word!

The prayer of our Savior impels us move on;
Its words are still sounding the call of our King;
And Paul, in devotion, doth echo the song,
"I beg you, my brethren, to speak the same thing."

Be faithful and true till the warfare is o'er,
Till factions are foiled and the vict'ry is won;
And millions of voices shall blend on the shore,
To welcome us enter our Father's glad home.

Chorus:
O shout the glad word, O hasten the day,
When all of God's people are one.
O shout the glad word, O hasten the day,
When all of God's people are one.

The hope for the end of division and the unity of all Christians is seen in this hymn.

> O shout the glad word,
> O hasten the day.

Let Party Names No More
S.M. Marshall(1856–1931) & M.C. Kurfrees

Let party names no more
The Christian world o'er-spread;
Gentile and Jew, and bond and free,
Are one in Christ, their head.

Among the saints on earth,
Let mutual love be found;
Heirs of the same inheritance,
With mutual blessings crowned.

Thus will the church below
Resemble that above;
Where streams of pleasure ever flow,
And every heart is love.

I found this hymn, dated 1887, in a tattered old hymnal while visiting friends in upstate Washington. It is a heartfelt appeal for the

Songs

assembled church on earth to resemble the church in heaven, where party names are no more.

Blest Be the Tie That Binds
John Fawcett (1740–1817)

Blest be the tie that binds,
Our hearts in Christian love;
The fellowship of kindred minds
Is like to that above.

Before our Father's throne,
We pour our ardent prayer;
Our fears, our hopes, our aims are one,
Our comforts and our cares.

We share our mutual woes,
Our mutual burdens bear;
And often for each other flows,
The sympathizing tear.

When we asunder part,
It gives us inward pain;
But we shall still be joined in heart,
And hope to meet again.

This touching song has surely been sung at the conclusion of more church gatherings than perhaps any other song. It brims with love and fellowship. The second stanza makes it clear that when we pray together we are one in our fears, hopes, aims, comforts, and cares.

> The fellowship of kindred minds Is like to that above.

Come, My Christian Friends and Brethren

Come, my Christian friends and brethren,
Bound for Canaan's happy land,
Come, unite and walk together,
Christ our leader gives command.

Lay aside your party spirit,
Wound your Christian friends no more,
All the name of Christ inherit,
Zion's peace again restore.

We'll not bind our brother's conscience,
This to God alone is free,
Nor contend with one another,
But in Christ united be:
Here's the Word, the grand criterion,
This shall all our doctrine prove,
Christ the centre of our union,
And the bond is Christian love.

Here my hand, my heart, my spirit,
Now in fellowship I give,
Now we'll love and peace inherit,
Show the world how Christians live;
We are one in Christ our Saviour,
Here is neither bond nor free,
Christ is all in all forever,
In His name we all agree.

Now we'll preach and pray together,
Praise, give thanks, and shout and sing;
Now we'll strengthen one another,
And adore our heavenly King;
Now we'll join in sweet communion,
Round the table of our Lord;
Lord, confirm our Christian union,
By Thy Spirit and Thy Word.

Now the world will be constrained
To believe in Christ our King;
Thousands, millions be converted,
Round the earth His praises ring;
Blessed day! O joyful hour!
Praise the Lord—His name we bless;

Send Thy kingdom, Lord, with pow'r,
Fill the world with righteousness.

Tom Lawson, a professor at Ozark Christian College, discovered this wonderful unity song in an 1829 hymnal published by Barton W. Stone and Thomas Adams, *The Christian Hymn-Book*. Lawson wrote in *One Body* (Summer 2003), "I am moved by the song's clarion call for unity and the strong connection drawn between working for unity and winning the world to Christ. . . . If the Stone-Campbell Movement ever wanted an 'anthem' of our own, I'd vote for this one." Lawson surmises that Stone himself may have written this hymn. Other researchers believe it to have been written by Stone's friend, Clement Nance (1757–1828). It has been sung to the tune of "Love Divine" at a number of unity meetings I have been involved with.

> We are one in Christ our Saviour,
> Here is neither bond nor free.

WHEN THE SAVIOR'S PRAYER IS ANSWERED
Carlton C. Buck (1907–)

When the Savior's prayer is answered,
Whether here or over there,
And at last the total victory is won,
Then the saints will be triumphant
With the joy of answered prayer,
Singing "Glory, Hallelujah to the Son!"

We can help to bring the answer
To the Savior's earnest prayer
By submitting to His good and perfect will.
We, the church can learn to follow,
And His yearnings we can share,
For in Heaven He is interceding still.

Jesus loves the church He founded,
Knew that Satan would assail,
And He prayed that all believers might be one.
Tho' He knew there would be hardship,

Yet the church would still prevail,
Finding oneness like the Father and the Son.

Chorus:
When the true church is together
In the final victory,
What a hymn of joyous triumph it will raise;
When the Savior's prayer is answered,
What rejoicing there will be,
All together, one in Christ, to sing His praise!

This newer hymn, written in 1988, appeared in *One Father, One Family* (Alger Fitch, College Press, 1990) and was also published in *One Body* (Fall 1994) with the author's kind permission. It

> When the Savior's prayer is answered, What rejoicing there will be.

speaks directly to the prayer of Jesus in John 17 and suggests that we have a part in answering His prayer.

CONTEMPORARY CHORUSES

The desire for oneness and togetherness in Christ is not limited to hymns from the past. Today there are many praise choruses that speak to the longing of Christians to be one, to be united, to be "together in Christ," to stand together, to worship together, to win the world for Christ together. The chorus titles alone are reflective of unity.

A Common Love (Charles F. Brown)
Bind Us Together (Bill Gillman)
The Bond of Love (Otis Skillings)
God's Family (Lanny Wolfe)
God's Wonderful People (Lanny Wolfe)
They'll Know We Are Christians by Our Love (Peter Scholtes)
Our God Has Made Us One (Niles Borop)
The Family of God (Gloria Gaither & William J. Gaither)
We Will Stand (Russ Taff & Tori Taff)
Let Us Break Bread Together (Traditional Spiritual)
Song for the Nations (Chris Christensen)

There is a common thread that runs through these wonderful choruses. We are blood-washed members of the family of God. We have been bonded together through the love of Christ. We are one in His name, one in His Spirit. Together we kneel in His presence to remember His broken body and shed blood, to seek His mercy. Together we rise from our knees to take our stand and sing His praises. Together we join our hearts and hands and work side by side until the whole world knows that we are Christians by our love for one another. As a result, others will come to know Christ and join us in the worship and work of our great King.

Classic hymns and contemporary choruses like these bring out the best in us. They make us want to be what God has always wanted us to be . . .

> together in Christ,
> > assembled in His presence,
> > > praising Him as one forever and ever!

O for a thousand Christians—and tens of thousands more—to lift our voices in song as one in praising our great Redeemer!

Chapter Four

THE CROSS, BAPTISM, AND THE LORD'S SUPPER

SYMBOLS OF UNITY

As my plane approached the shoreline of New York City, I could see the form of the famous lady in the harbor looming large in the late afternoon sun. It was November 1990 and I was returning from my first visit to Poland. For two weeks I had traveled all over Poland, teaching, preaching, visiting churches and other places. I shall never forget my visit to Auschwitz-Birkenau where a million or more Jews, who had been forced to wear the yellow Star of David, the symbol of Judaism, perished in that man-made hell. I talked to a survivor whose entire family "went up the smokestack." But the hated and dreaded symbol of Nazism, the swastika, no longer cast its sinister shadow over Auschwitz. And Poland itself was no longer in the grip of communism. I saw some of the last Russian troops, who had occupied Poland since the infamous decision at Yalta, preparing to return to the former USSR. No longer would the hammer and the sickle be seen in Poland, except in documentary films. How glad I was to return to America, "land of the free." The next day I visited the Statue of Liberty, climbing the winding stairs to her very top. I thanked God for the freedoms I had enjoyed for years but had taken for granted.

> I shall never forget my visit to Auschwitz-Birkenau where a million or more Jews perished in that man-made hell.

The Star of David. The swastika. The hammer and sickle. The Statue of Liberty. All of these are symbols, visual representations of reality—for good or evil. The word "symbol" comes from the Greek language: *syn* (together), *ballein* (to throw). A symbol is an emblem, token, sign, or figure that stands for something. It is a visible representation of reality.

59

In the Old Testament, there are a number of significant symbols. When Adam and Eve were banished from the beautiful Garden of Eden, God placed cherubim east of Eden, and a *flaming sword* which rotated 360 degrees, evidently to prevent the fallen couple from returning to the tree of life (Gen. 3:24). The flaming sword is a symbol of man's failure to obey God.

The story of the Great Flood includes at least three items which have become symbols. When the ark rested on the mountains of Ararat (located in modern-day Turkey), Noah sent out a *dove* to see if the waters had receded. But the dove could find no resting-place, and returned to the ark. After seven days, Noah again sent the dove in search of dry land. At evening the dove returned, this time with a freshly plucked *olive leaf* in her mouth (Gen. 8:11). Today the olive branch is an international symbol of peace, just as the olive leaf in Noah's day could be seen as a symbol of renewed peace between God and man. The flag of the United Nations features a map of the world surrounded by a wreath made of olive branches. In the New Testament, the dove is symbolic of the Holy Spirit who descended upon Christ at His baptism in the Jordan River (Matt. 3:16). Yet a third symbol appears in the account of the flood, the *rainbow*. God told Noah, "I set My rainbow in the cloud, and it shall be for the sign of the covenant between Me and the earth" (Gen. 9:13). God assured Noah that never again would He destroy all flesh by means of a worldwide flood. The rainbow is a visible reminder of that promise made to Noah.

The story of the Passover is rich in visual representations. When the Israelites were doing slave labor in Egypt, God, through Moses, told them to take a *lamb* for their household (Exod. 12:3). The lamb had to be a male, without blemish, and kept in the house until the 14th of Nisan (April), when it was to be killed at twilight. In the New Testament, Christ is the Lamb of God, slain for the sins of the world (John 1:29; Rev. 5:6). The *blood* of the sacrificial lamb then was to be sprinkled on the doorpost and lintel of the house. God said, "Now the blood shall be a sign for you on the houses where you are. And when I see the blood, I will pass over you; and the plague shall not be on you to destroy you when I strike the land of Egypt" (Exod. 12:13).

Following the Exodus from Egypt, Israel was instructed to build the *tabernacle*, a kind of "portable church" for the nation (Exod. 26–40). The tabernacle was a type, or symbol, of Christ and heaven, according to the book of Hebrews. It was divided into two parts: the *holy place* and the *most holy place (or Holy of Holies)*. Within the holy place were such things as *a golden lampstand* (presence of God's Spirit), *table of showbread* (symbolic of God's provision for His people), and *altar of incense* (representative of the prayers of the people ascending to God), while inside the Holy of Holies were the *Ark of the Covenant* [containing a second set of the *Ten Commandments* (God's law, also God the Father), *golden pot of manna* (God's provision, also God the Son, the Bread of Heaven), and *Aaron's rod* (God's power, also the Holy Spirit)] and the *Mercy Seat* (God's presence) atop the Ark of the Covenant. Outside the tabernacle itself, in the outer court, was the *altar of burnt offering* (our sacrificial commitment) and the *bronze laver* (the necessity for purification before entering God's presence).

During the forty years of wandering in the wilderness, the Israelites began to foolishly speak against God and Moses. A plague of fiery serpents followed and many people died. God instructed Moses to make a *bronze serpent* and place it on a pole. Anyone who had been bitten by the poisonous snakes, if they looked upon the bronze serpent, would live (Num. 21:8,9). Jesus repeated this symbolic story in reference to His own impending death on the cross (John 3:14,15). He was the healing serpent raised up on a pole for everyone to look at and be healed. The bronze serpent entwined around a staff of the Israelites existed long before the Asklepios (single snake on a staff) and Caduceus (two snakes on a staff) of Greek mythology, standing symbols of the pharmaceutical and medical practices.

All of these indicate that God uses symbols to communicate abstract ideas to us. He gives us many "pictures" to help us understand His relationship with us and the world. Likewise, He gives us symbols to unify us, to draw us together as brothers and sisters in Christ, so that we will be reminded of our need for and dependence on one another.

When Israel finally crossed over the Jordan River and entered into the Promised Land, God, through Joshua, instructed them to build an **altar** of twelve stones, one stone for each of the twelve tribes (Josh. 3:3). The altar was to remind future generations that God allowed them to cross over on dry land. It was also a powerful symbol of Israel's unity—twelve tribes yet "one nation, under God."

Our next illustration of biblical symbols in the Old Testament is the **two sticks** that became **one stick** in the hands of Ezekiel during the Babylonian Captivity. The prophet was told to take two sticks (representing Judah and Israel, the divided kingdoms), place them together, and "they will become one in your hand" (Ezek. 38:17); but more than that, they would become one in *God's* hand (Ezek. 38:19). God said He would make them into "one nation" serving under "one king," and they would never "be divided into two kingdoms again" (Ezek. 37:22). This, perhaps, is the greatest symbol of unity in the Old Testament, to be eclipsed only by the two beams of wood that fashioned the cross of Christ.

Before we look at biblical symbols of Christian unity in the New Testament, let us "fast forward" into the postapostolic age. One of the most famous symbols of Christianity, **the sign of the fish**, should be considered. The Greek letters ΙΧΘΥΣ formed an acrostic: *Jesus Christ, Son of God, Savior*. This symbol is seen in many places yet today, from Bible covers to the backs of automobiles. But in the early centuries of Christianity, the symbol of the fish could be found scratched on the outer walls or doors of houses occupied by believers. It is thought to have been a marking indicating that the Lord's Supper would be secretly observed in that house that night. It allowed Christians to know where they could seek out other brothers in a time when it was dangerous to be a Christian.

There are at least three symbols of Christian unity revealed to us in the New Testament. They stand today, as they have for centuries, as beautiful and meaningful symbols—visible representations of reality. They are **the cross, baptism**, and **the Lord's Supper**. Charles R. Gresham has observed that Christian unity was created at the

> Christian unity was created at the cross, appropriated at baptism, and remembered in the Lord's Supper.

cross, appropriated at baptism, and remembered in the Lord's Supper (*One Body,* July 1985).

The Cross of Christ

In his book *The Cross of Christ* (InterVarsity Press, 1986), John R.W. Stott writes that every religion or ideology has its visual symbol.

Judaism has the Star of David, Islam the crescent moon, Buddhism the lotus flower. Stott says there could have been a wide range of possibilities that Christians could have chosen as their symbol, including the manger, the dove, the empty tomb, or a throne. But by the time of the second century it became clear that the cross was the pictorial symbol of their faith (the crucifix, according to Stott, did not appear as Christianity's symbol until the sixth century).

Several years ago I took part in a panel discussion on "The Shape of Unity." The moderator said, "Every shape has lines that distinguish it—what is inside and what is outside. Give us a biblical definition of the shape of Christian unity." I chose the shape of the cross. I said, "There is salvation, safety, and security within the lines of the cross. But beyond the shape of the cross there is haughtiness, hopelessness, and hell itself. Inside the cross there is light and laughter. Outside the cross there is darkness and despair. The cross of Christ glows like a candle in the night, sends out a ray of hope like a lighthouse in the stormy darkness, and reigns in majesty over all the earth like the blazing star of Bethlehem."

> The cross of Christ is both the symbol and shape of Christian unity.

The cross of Christ is both the symbol and shape of Christian unity. God, righteous and holy, met man, sinful and lost, at the cross. In our sin we could not meet God and so a mediator appeared on the scene. "For there is one God and one Mediator between God and men, the Man Christ Jesus, who gave Himself a ransom for all . . . ." (1 Tim. 2:5,6). In this case, the mediator did not just mediate—He

63

gave His life as a ransom for sinners. "And for this reason He is the Mediator of the new covenant, by means of death, for the redemption of the transgressions under the first covenant, that those who are called may receive the promise of eternal inheritance" (Heb. 9:15). Samuel Rutherford observed, "The cross of Christ, on which he was extended, points, in the length of it, to heaven and earth, reconciling them together; and in the breadth of it, to former and following ages, as being equally salvation to both."

We have been *redeemed* through the blood of Christ shed on the cross (Eph. 1:7; Col. 1:14), and we also have been *reconciled* through that same precious blood. In fact, the reconciliation is dual in nature. We have been "reconciled to God through the death of His Son" (Rom. 5:10), and we have been reconciled to each other when Christ "made peace through the blood of His cross" (Col. 1:20,21).

The cross of Christ is a symbol of unity, not only between God and man but also between those who have been mortal enemies with each other. With reference to Jew and Gentile, Paul wrote, "For he himself is our peace, who has made the two one and has destroyed the barrier, the dividing wall of hostility. . . . His purpose was to create in himself one new man out of the two, thus making peace, and in this one body to reconcile both of them to God through the cross, by which he put to death their hostility" (Eph. 2:14-16, NIV). This work of reconciliation has already been accomplished at the cross. Just as we have "received the atonement" (Rom. 5:11), we must be willing to receive the reconciliation. Paul put it this way: "Therefore receive one another, just as Christ also received us, to the glory of God" (Rom. 15:7). How do some justify their practice of rejecting those whom Christ has received? If Jesus reconciled us to each other by making peace through the blood of His cross (Col. 1:20,21), it is a terrible affront to Christ and His blood to refuse to receive the reconciliation!

Erwin Lutzer noted, "The purpose of the cross is to repair the irreparable." The cross of Christ not only reconciles sinful man with a holy God, it also reconciles the estranged with each other. The reconciling power of the cross is first vertical, then horizontal. The cross of Christ is

> The cross of Christ is not only a ladder to heaven, but is also a bridge to peace.

not only a ladder to heaven, but is also a bridge to peace. Isn't it time to cross that bridge?

The Waters of Baptism

Many people who go to church today are looking for something that is relevant and experiential. There are few things more visual, relevant, and experiential in the practice of the church than baptism and the Lord's Supper. This section will deal with the subject of baptism.

Recently Timothy George, executive editor of *Christianity Today*, answered a question from a reader in his column "Good Question": "What is the role of baptism in faith and salvation?" George responded, in part, "Baptism must take place in the context of faith, and it must connect to the central events of the gospel—Jesus' cross and resurrection" (*CT*, July 2003). This is precisely the point Paul made in Romans 6 when he asked, "Or don't you know that all of us who were baptized into Christ Jesus were baptized into his death? We were therefore buried with him through baptism into death in order that, just as Christ was raised from the dead through the glory of the Father, we too may live a new life. If we have been united with him like this in his

> "Baptism must take place in the context of faith, and it must connect to the central events of the gospel— Jesus' cross and resurrection."

death, we will certainly also be united with him in his resurrection" (Rom. 6:3-5, NIV). Baptism certainly connects to the central events of the gospel! When we are "baptized into Christ Jesus," we are "baptized into his death." Following our being "buried with him through baptism into death" and our being "united with him like this in his death," we are "united with him in his resurrection."

This passage in Romans is more clearly understood when placed alongside what Paul wrote to the Corinthians when he defined the gospel. He declared, "that Christ died for our sins according to the Scriptures, that he was buried, that he was raised on the third day according to the Scriptures" (1 Cor. 15:3,4, NIV). The *gospel*, therefore, is the death, burial, and resurrection of our Lord—as it is portrayed in Scripture. Our *response* to the gospel is our death, burial, and resurrection—as it is portrayed in Christian baptism.

Martin Luther once said, "Your baptism is nothing less than grace clutching you by the throat: a grace-full throttling, by which your sin is submerged in order that ye remain under grace. Come thus to thy baptism. Give thyself up to be drowned in baptism and killed by the mercy of thy dear God, saying, 'Drown me and throttle me, dear Lord, for henceforth I will gladly die to sin with thy Son'" (as quoted in *Down in the River to Pray*, John Mark Hicks & Greg Taylor, Leafwood Publishers, 2003).

Every case of conversion in the Book of Acts culminated in the baptism of the believer. Convicted by the Holy Spirit-inspired preaching of the apostles, believers repented of their sins, confessed their faith in Christ, and were immersed in the waters of baptism. They did not balk at baptism. They did not belittle baptism. They did not bide their time to be baptized. Baptism was the normative experience for those who turned from sin to Christ in the New Testament era. From the Day of Pentecost onward, baptism was always an immediate faith response to the gospel of grace.

> From the Day of Pentecost onward, baptism was always an immediate faith response to the gospel of grace.

In his book *Baptism Today and Tomorrow* (St. Martin's Press, 1966), G.R. Beasley-Murray finds five attendant blessings to baptism in the New Testament:

- Forgiveness of sins (Acts 2:38; 22:16)
- Union with Christ (Gal. 3:26; Col. 2:12; Rom. 6:1-11)
- Possession of the Holy Spirit (Acts 2:38; Titus 3:5)
- Membership in the church (1 Cor. 12:13)
- Inheritance in the kingdom of God (John 3:5)

Beasley-Murray concludes, "In the light of these statements I am compelled to conclude that the understanding of baptism as 'a beautiful and expressive symbol,' *and nothing more,* is irreconcilable with the New Testament." Baptism is a symbol of our union with Christ, but it is more than merely a symbol. It is a dynamic action, an actual participation, a life-changing event. In baptism we are buried *with Christ,* immersed into *His death.* There, beneath the water, we die with Him. Coming up out of the water we are raised with Him. The saving power in this act of faith is linked to the resurrection of Christ. "And this water symbolizes baptism that now saves you also—not the removal of dirt from the body but the pledge of a good conscience toward God. It saves you by the resurrection of Jesus Christ" (1 Pet. 3:21, NIV). Baptism is a tremendous act of faith that God is graciously doing something special to us and for us. "Having been buried with him in baptism and raised with him through your faith in the power of God, who raised him from the dead" (Col. 2:12).

> Baptism is more than merely a symbol. It is a dynamic action, an actual participation, a life-changing event.

Baptism not only unites us with Christ but also with every other immersed believer, past and present. Paul reminded the church in Corinth, "For by one Spirit we were all baptized into one body—whether Jews or Greeks, whether slaves or free—and have all been made to drink into one Spirit. For in fact the body is not one member but many" (1 Cor. 12:13). Baptism, therefore, is the threshold of entrance into the church as well as to Christ. "For you are all sons of God through faith in Christ Jesus. For as many of you as were baptized into Christ have put on Christ. There is neither Jew nor Greek, there is neither slave nor free, there is neither male nor female; for you are all one in Christ Jesus" (Gal. 3:26-28).

I was reminded of baptism being a symbol of our unity in Christ when I visited Ukraine in 2004. The believers there had suffered great persecution under the communists. The Soviets had passed a law forbidding baptism to anyone under the age of twenty-one unless the church provided the local government with a list of those who desired to be baptized. The communist officials would determine who would be baptized and those who would not! Some churches went along with the decree but others (those I visited) did not. Nearly every preacher in their fellowship had spent time in prison because of their refusal to obey the ban on baptism. Some did not return but died in prison or hard labor camps. One day we crossed a river that is called "Baptism River" to this day. Here is where hundreds of believers came, at the risk of persecution and imprisonment, to be baptized into union with Christ and other penitent believers. I felt a kinship with all those, past and present, who had been baptized in this river into union with Christ and with every other penitent believer in Christ of every era.

On another occasion, this time in Belarus, I witnessed the baptism of penitent believers in a river that flowed beneath a large bridge in a large city. On one side of the river were the believers, a thousand strong. On the other side of the river were unbelievers, scores of them seated on the grass. On the bridge spanning the river, traffic had stopped and people had gotten out of their cars to observe the proceedings below. It was a vivid reminder that baptism is the dividing line, the line of demarcation, between the Christian and the world. When we are baptized into Christ, we are added to the number of believers (Acts 2:41). We not only belong to Jesus Christ, we belong to each other. We are the baptized body of Christ! In baptism we find ourselves "together in Christ!"

> Baptism is the dividing line, the line of demarcation, between the Christian and the world.

The Lord's Supper

I never feel closer to the worldwide body of Christ than at Communion. There is something that takes place in the observance of the Lord's Supper, "the crown jewel of worship," that does not happen in praise, preaching, or prayer. I sense a glad, gripping, global connection with all of God's far-flung family.

Paul was in Ephesus when he wrote to the church in Corinth, located on the narrow isthmus between the Aegean and Adriatic Seas. The surging waters could not separate Paul in Ephesus from the believers in Corinth. They were one in spirit. And so Paul wrote, "The cup of blessing which we bless, is it not the communion of the blood of Christ? The bread which we break, is it not the communion of the body of Christ? For we, being many, are one bread and one body; for we all partake of that one bread" (1 Cor. 10:16,17).

We are one bread and one body. Especially in the weekly observance of the Lord's Supper. It is a symbol of our unity in Christ, and yet it seems more than just a symbol when believers break bread together. "The bread which we break, is it not the communion of the body of Christ?" Of course it is. The New International Version uses the word "participation." That's what it is—an actual, experiential participation!

We should never partake of the communion emblems without first "discerning the Lord's body" (1 Cor. 11:29). What is the Lord's body? First, it is His body, broken on the cross for us (1 Cor. 11:24). It is through His shed blood that we have the forgiveness of our sins. But the Lord's body is also . . . *us.* We are the visible body of Christ today. Paul writes, "Now you are the body of Christ" (1 Cor. 12:27). We do partake of the bread and cup in remembrance of Christ, as He asked (Luke 22:19). We can also partake of the sacred emblems in recognition of the body of Christ—His worldwide church, for the church is His body (Eph. 1:22,23).

> The Lord's Day without the Lord's Supper is like a beautiful rose without the fragrance.

The Lord's Day without the Lord's Supper is like a beautiful rose without the fragrance. When I partake of the bread and cup, I do so in remembrance of Christ. It reminds me of my union with Him, as Gresham said, "created at the cross, appropriated at baptism, remembered at the Lord's Supper." But I can also do so in recognition of His beloved body—baptized believers girdling the globe. Jesus died for them too. And some of them are dying for Him, even as I partake! Did not Paul say that the cup is the communion of the blood of Christ? The body of Christ continues to shed blood—not as an act of atonement but in moments of martyrdom. Fulton J. Sheen wrote, "Bread is made from a multiplicity of grains of wheat, and . . . has to pass through the rigors of winter, be ground beneath the Calvary of a mill, and then subjected to purging fire before it can become bread" (*Life of Christ,* McGraw-Hill, 1958).

I recall a communion service on the beautiful island of Cuba in 1996. It was Sunday evening in old Havana, and more than 100

Symbols

believers were crowded into a small stucco house and its adjoining courtyard. The communist authorities frown on house churches that assemble in groups of more than twenty. In spite of government informants on the block, the Christians sang with joy—and volume! When it became evident that not enough bread and grape juice was available, they gladly shared their tiny cube of bread (dividing it with their fingernails) and their little cup of grape juice so that all could partake and none would feel left out. The Lord's Supper is something to be shared, something the church in Corinth forgot.

In a small, cold room off the sanctuary in St. Margaret's Church in London, we ate the bread and drank the cup with several dozen hardy believers. London's great cathedrals are full during the week (with tourists) but are nearly devoid of worshipers on Sunday. But here we were one—and felt very much one—as we shared in the Lord's Supper.

In "Bloody Belfast," Northern Ireland, where thousands have died in religious violence, I was touched by "the prayers of the church" that ascended from the elder's lips to the heavenly throne—intercessions for the needs of Belfast as well as other sufferers in the world. The Lord's Supper was spread in the old Berlin Street church in a manner most solemn. Detractors would call it "high church," but I felt the Spirit of God descend as we broke the bread and drank the cup.

"Down under," in the land of the Southern Cross, I assembled with Australians and New Zealanders to "discern the body." The morning service was strictly for believers and I was blessed as the presiders stood behind the Lord's Table and read first from the Old Testament and then from the Gospels. The evening service was for unbelievers and after my sermon we took a young man to be baptized in the moon-lit South Pacific Ocean. The body of Christ had just grown by one, "for by one Spirit are we all baptized into one body" (1 Cor. 12:13).

One year after the Berlin Wall came down, I found myself in northern Poland, on the Baltic Sea. The wall was down, the Table was spread, and believers from East and West were one at long last. Together in Christ as they have always been. The chalice was cold, but my heart was strangely warmed. On the front wall of the church, right behind the Lord's Table and just to the right of the wooden cross are beautifully engraved words, *OTO PRZYJDE WKROTCE . . .* "Behold, I am coming quickly" (Rev. 22:12).

> The wall was down, the Table was spread, and believers from East and West were one at long last.

He is at that. And that right soon. In the meantime, "For as often as you eat this bread and drink the cup, you proclaim the Lord's death until He comes" (1 Cor. 11:26). Until He comes! We do not think of Christ's second coming nearly enough. But the weekly observance of the Lord's Supper reminds us that Jesus is coming again. Every Lord's Supper could be our Last Supper.

Come quickly, Lord Jesus. May you find us:
together in You,
meeting around Your table,
filled with Your love for one another.

Chapter Five

"IN ESSENTIALS, UNITY"
SLOGANS ON UNITY

The advertising world knows the power of slogans. Many of you could finish the following without any trouble because the slogans are so familiar to you.

✛ "Can you hear me . . ."
✛ "Good to the very last . . ."
✛ "You deserve a . . ."
✛ "It's the real . . ."
✛ "Where's the . . ."
✛ "Just do . . ." *

A slogan is a maxim or adage that has come from the collected wisdom of the ages; a truth that has withstood the test of time. "Haste makes waste." "A stitch in time saves nine." "A rolling stone gathers no moss." "Better safe than sorry." "I have a dream." "Give me liberty or give me death." "Ask not what your country can do for you; ask what you can do for your country."

For those who have made the unity of all believers a priority in their lives, slogans have been used to encapsulate this noble desire. A slogan, it should be noted, should never be put on par with Scripture. A slogan, no matter how truthful or sensible, is still a creation of man's mind and thinking.

> For those who have made the unity of all believers a priority in their lives, slogans have been used to encapsulate this noble desire.

---

* "now?" (Verizon Wireless); "drop" (Maxwell House Coffee); "break today" (McDonald's); "thing" (Coca-Cola); "beef?" (Wendy's); "it" (Nike).

The word origin of "slogan" in itself is interesting. It comes from the Highland clans of Scotland, from the Scottish Gaelic: *slugah* (army) and *garim* (battle cry, rallying cry). In this chapter we are using slogan in the sense of a *rallying* cry, not a *battle* cry! The selected slogans that will follow have been used as a rallying cry to call believers everywhere to unity—a unity that is based upon the Word of God and centered in Jesus Christ.

SLOGANS EMPHASIZING CHRISTIAN UNITY

A famous slogan that has been used for centuries is: *"In essentials, unity; in opinions, liberty; in all things, charity."* This motto has been ascribed to a seventeenth-century Lutheran theologian, Peter Meiderlin who sometimes used the pen name, Rupertus Meldenius. The slogan has taken on various forms. "In matters of faith, unity; in matters of opinion, liberty; in all things, love." Richard Baxter (1615–1691) said, "In necessary things, unity; in doubtful things, liberty; in all things, charity." On January 1, 1906, the first evangelical Christian publication was produced in Russia. Founder and editor Ivan S. Prokhanov included a variation of this slogan on the masthead: "In essential things, unity; in secondary things, freedom; in all things, charity." Prokhanov's goal was "the unification of all the branches of living Christianity on the principles of freedom and brotherly love" (*In the Cauldron of Russia,* One Body Ministries, 1993). In the mid-twentieth century, the *Christian-Evangelist* had it this way on their masthead: "In essentials, unity; in opinions and methods, liberty; in all things, love." For many years Meiderlin's motto also appeared on the masthead of *Pulpit Helps,* a monthly preaching journal sent to thousands of evangelical preachers in America. Hans Kung says Pope John XXIII never tired of saying, "*In necessariis, unitas; in dubiis, libertas, in omnibus autem, caritas*" ("In necessary things, unity; in doubtful things, freedom, but in everything, love").

> An "essential" is a matter of fact, but more than that, a matter of faith.

Something which is "essential" is that which is indispensable. Water, food, and air are essential to life. Spiritual life also has its essentials. An "essential" is a matter of fact, but more than that, a matter of faith. This slogan says that we should strive for unity in those things that are of "first importance." While all truths are equally true, all truths are not of equal importance. Paul wrote, "For what I received I passed on to you as of first importance: that Christ died for our sins according to the Scriptures, that he was buried, that he was raised on the third day according to the Scriptures" (1 Cor. 15:3,4, NIV). The death, burial, and resurrection of Christ are the very essence of the gospel. They are matters of fact *and* matters of faith. John Newton said, "Paul was a reed in non-essentials, an iron pillar in essentials." We must pray for wisdom to know the difference between essentials and nonessentials; for strength to stand like an iron pillar; for humility to sway like a reed.

> "Paul was a reed in non-essentials, an iron pillar in essentials."

Some say we cannot make distinctions—that *everything* in Scripture, because it is Scripture, must be viewed as essential. But those who take this view soon become bogged down in their efforts to apply all of Scripture to the church and the Christian life. Their circle of fellowship narrows and narrows until they find themselves pretty much alone—something God never intended. The view that makes everything in Scripture a matter of faith is impractical and leads to legalism. But we do not want to take the opposing view—that everything in Scripture is a matter of opinion. This view is untenable and leads to liberalism. It leaves us a message with no teeth; worse, no heart. How can we possibly say that the death of Christ does not atone for sin or that Jesus did not bodily arise from the grave? We do not want to be numbered with those who would make what is clearly a hallmark of faith a bookmark of opinion.

The problem in applying the principle contained in this slogan is that we have not been able to agree on what is essential and what is nonessential, but that does not mean we should cease in trying to come to a consensus on matters of faith. There are Scriptures that seem to be very clear in what is essential. Ephesians 4:4-6, containing seven unities, is one such passage. Paul

> We do not want to be numbered with those who would make what is clearly a hallmark of faith a bookmark of opinion.

75

clearly states that there is one body, one Spirit, one hope, one Lord, one faith, one baptism, and one God and Father of all. Surely that is a worthy platform for unity. Other Scriptures, by their use of words like "unless," "except," and "must" would also be an indicator of an essential. ". . . unless you repent, you will all likewise perish" (Luke 13:5). "Unless you believe that I am He, you shall die in your sins" (John 8:24, NASB). ". . . unless one is born of water and the Spirit, he cannot enter the kingdom of God" (John 3:5). "You must be born again" (John 3:7). Surely those have to be included in the "essentials."

The essentials, it would seem, would center in the central theme of the Bible: God's redemptive love as accomplished in His Son's death on the cross for the salvation of a lost world. Knofel Staton, in paraphrasing a statement made by Thomas Campbell in his "Declaration and Address," wrote, "It is not necessary that people see *all* God's truth exactly alike before they are added to His Church. What is necessary is that they recognize two things: (1) their lost condition and (2) Jesus' way of salvation. And then declare their faith in Him and their willingness to obey Him in all things." W. Carl Ketcherside said, "Make nothing a test of fellowship that God has not made a condition of salvation." We dare not make primary what is clearly secondary.

> We dare not make primary what is clearly secondary.

J.S. Lamar offered a three-pronged approach to distinguishing between the essential and the nonessential. He believed that there were things essential, things important, and things indifferent. Things essential, according to Lamar, were "the absolute essentials of objective Christianity"—"the reception of which makes a man a Christian." While the essentials are designed to *impart* life, things important are for *nourishing and developing* that life. Things essential *make* us Christians while things important make us better, wiser, stronger Christians. Things indifferent, in Lamar's judgment, are of much lesser importance. He included such things as certain matters of public worship where "all parties search the Scriptures for authority, pro and con, and finding none, as, of course, they do not, the matter not being the subject of Scripture teaching at all, strain and force different texts into a sort of simulated support of their respective position, while heart-burnings, uncharitable speeches, and all manner of evil thoughts grow and multiply . . ." (*New Testament Christianity,* Vol. I, 1923).

In matters of opinion (secondary things, doubtful things) we will never unite. But we should never reject a brother for whom Christ died or a sister whom God has accepted (Rom. 14:1-4). Liberty and freedom must be extended, given, and allowed. Most important of all, love must be manifested—for without love we are nothing, zip, zilch, zero, *nada.*

Another unity slogan is *"Union in truth."* This comes to us from Thomas Campbell in his "Declaration and Address," issued in 1809. He wrote, "Union in truth has been, and ever must be, the desire and prayer of all; 'Union in truth' is our motto." Leroy Garrett comments, "In view of the context of the document, it is evident that he meant that their plea for unity was based upon the great truths of the Christian faith—not upon opinions, theories, or theologies, and certainly not upon the creeds of men. He was really saying 'Unity in *the* Truth,' that (which) is the truth centered in Jesus Christ, or the core gospel" (*One Body,* Winter 2003). That Campbell meant biblical truth is made clear by the next sentence following "'Union in truth' is our motto" for it reads, "The Divine word is our standard; in the Lord's name do we display our banners."

This slogan is based upon the prayer of Jesus in John 17:20,21, "I do not pray for these alone, but also for those who will believe in Me *through their word*; that they all may be one. . . ." True Christian unity is centered in Christ and entrenched in truth, especially the truth that Jesus Christ is who He claimed to be and accomplished what He said He would do. "Consequently, faith comes from hearing the message, and the message is heard through the word of Christ" (Rom. 10:17, NIV). What the apostles preached about Christ was the true word of God (1 Thess. 2:13). There can be no Christian unity that is not centered on Christ and entrenched in truth. Some today surrender truth for "unity" (and some even sacrifice unity for "truth"), but Thomas Campbell insisted, rightly, that "union in truth" should be our motto.

A third unity slogan comes to us from Barton W. Stone, who said, *"Let Christian unity be our polar star."* This slogan, too, seems to

> There can be no Christian unity that is not centered on Christ and entrenched in truth.

have been based upon Jesus' famous prayer for unity in John 17:21, ". . . that they all may be one, as You, Father, are in Me, and I in You; that they also may be one in Us, that the world may believe that You sent Me."

The North Star (sometimes called Polaris, polestar, or polar star) is permanently fixed in the heavens. It doesn't move around but is constantly in the same place all the time so that it can serve as a fixed point or guide. Stone believed our unity *in Christ* was the polar star. "Jesus Christ is the same yesterday, today, and forever" (Heb. 13:8). He is our unchanging, never-moving, always-reliable guide. *Christian* unity, therefore, will keep us on track. Unity in Christ is more, much more, than an end in itself. It keeps us on course so that we may lead others to Christ for salvation.

Another motto that emphasizes Christian unity is this one: ***"We are free to differ, but not to divide."*** While its origin is uncertain (probably mid-20th century), its message is a worthy one. W.T. Moore said it was intended to keep us united as a unity movement. As noted, we are bound to have differences in matters of opinion. In these (opinions, disputable matters, secondary things) we should especially strive to apply this motto—"free to differ, but not to divide." Leroy Garret comments, "The slogan reflects the basis upon which the Stone and Campbell movement united in 1832. They had their differences—just as Stone and Campbell did—but they united on the 'essentials' they held in common. The slogan also points to their disdain for division among Christians—'a horrid evil' as Thomas Campbell put it. In this slogan they were saying that since division is sinful we are not free to divide, even though we have our differences. It is a factious spirit that divides, not honest differences" (ibid.).

A divided church is a terrible witness to the world. "Is Christ divided?" (1 Cor. 1:13). No. Should His church, His body, be divided? The answer is obvious. We can (and will) have our differences in nonessentials. This slogan says we are free to differ. But in the essentials, the things that matter for eternity, let us have unity. For Christ's sake and for the world's sake, let us never divide!

The importance of Scripture has already been alluded to in some of the slogans we have already considered, especially Thomas Campbell's mention of "Union *in truth.*" Campbell was known as a "Man of the Book" because of strong belief that people could be Christians only if they accepted the Bible, God's Holy Word, the truth, as their only rule of faith and practice. In 1809 he called for the abandonment of everything in religion for which there was no biblical basis. ***"Where the Scriptures speak, we speak; and where the Scriptures are silent, we are silent."*** Robert Richardson said of this slogan, "Henceforth, the plain and simple teaching of the Word of God itself was to be their guide. God himself should speak to them, and they should receive and repeat his words alone. No remote inferences, no fanciful interpretations, no religious theories of any kind, were to be allowed to alter or pervert its obvious meaning" (*Memoirs of Alexander Campbell,* Gospel Advocate Co., 1956).

Campbell was saying that Scripture was the all-sufficient norm for Christians. The reformers called it *sola Scriptura,* Scripture alone. Scripture itself makes the claim that it is sufficient. "All Scripture is inspired by God and profitable for teaching, for reproof, for correction, for training in righteousness; that the man of God may be adequate, equipped for every good work" (2 Tim. 3:16,17, NASB). If we are going to speak, let us speak what God has spoken. "If anyone speaks, let him speak as the oracles of God" (1 Pet. 4:11). "Oracle" is a diminutive of *logos,* denoting a divine response or utterance. Campbell was saying let our speaking, teaching, preaching, even writing be the essence of what God has already spoken in His Word. "Forever, O Lord, Your word is settled in heaven" (Ps. 119:89).

And when God does not speak? Where has God not spoken? Campbell continued, "And where the Scriptures are silent, we are silent." In other words, if God has not spoken on a subject, we should not. We should keep quiet about those things on which Scripture (God) says nothing. But too many times we have failed to remain silent. We have become very vocal on many matters—matters that the Scriptures do not address clearly and convincingly. Silence has no

> Silence has no authority whatsoever. Silence means "forbearance from speech." Silence must always yield to "that which is written."

authority whatsoever. Silence means "forbearance from speech." Silence must always yield to "that which is written." We cannot (and should not) speak with any authority where God has not spoken. Where God has spoken, let us speak that truth in love. Where God has not spoken, let us resist the temptation to speak.

Closely aligned with the above slogan, yet expanding into other areas, is the slogan of unknown origin which reads, *"No book but the Bible, no creed but Christ, no name but the divine."* Sometimes a fourth phrase is added, "no law but love" (similar to the "in all things, love" of Peter Meiderlin). We will examine the "No book but the Bible" segment here and look at the rest of this slogan in the section following.

By saying "No book but the Bible" those who seek Christian unity are saying that the Bible is the only reliable guide. Thomas Campbell put it this way: "The Bible is the only rule of faith and practice for Christians." Barton W. Stone said, "We will, that the people henceforth take the Bible as the only sure guide to heaven. . . ." And why not? Only the Bible can claim inspiration from God (2 Tim. 3:16), freedom from error (Titus 1:2), and the power to save (2 Tim. 3:15). Other books (like prayer books, hymnbooks, Bible commentaries) may be helpful, but only the Good Book is "living and active" (Heb. 4:12) which "effectively works" in the life of believers (1 Thess. 2:13). Sometimes small groups can even focus more on a study guide than the Bible itself. What men say about the Bible is important, but what God says about man in the Bible is imperative.

A motto that is mentioned several times in Marshall Leggett's book *Introduction to the Restoration Ideal* (Standard Publishing, 1986), is, *"Let us do Bible things in Bible ways, and call Bible things by Bible names."* The idea here is that for something to be biblical, it must be in the Bible. If the Bible calls baptism a burial (Rom. 6:4), then let all who come to Christ be buried in baptism with Him. If followers of Christ were called Christians (Acts 11:26), then let us call ourselves Christians. Leggett says, "The plea is for all to become Christians as they follow the Bible, striving to restore the church as it was given to the apostles and seeking the lost with the simple plan of salvation."

The *spirit* of the Bible, however, has sometimes been overlooked by those contending for "the Bible only." Barton W. Stone said, "The scriptures will never keep together in union and fellowship members not in the spirit of the scriptures, which spirit is love, peace, unity, forbearance, and cheerful obedience. This is the spirit of the great Head of the body." We must avoid the danger of becoming sectarian in opposing sectarianism.

> "The scriptures will never keep together in union and fellowship members not in the spirit of the scriptures."

When I was preaching for the Norvale Park Church in Eugene, Oregon, in the early 1970s, we used a slogan in our church paper that read, *"All we need is the Bible, but we need all of the Bible."* This motto meant that *all* Scripture was inspired of God and useful for teaching—the Old Testament Scriptures as well as the New Testament writings. Some put it this way: the Old Testament is the New Testament concealed while the New Testament is the Old Testament revealed. The Messianic prophecies of the Old Testament are fulfilled in Christ. It is easier to understand Revelation if you are familiar with the writings of Daniel. Or the thought may be that we cannot lift verses out of context and start a new religion on just a few passages. We need the Bible as a whole. "The best commentary on the Bible is the Bible itself," is how some put it.

Yet another slogan emphasizing the importance of Scripture is this one: *"The Bible only makes Christians only."* The thought here is that the Bible *plus* some other book or creed would make a Christian *plus* something else. Since the Bible does not speak of "hyphenated" Christians (Baptist-Christians, Methodist-Christians, Presbyterian-Christians, etc.), we should seek to be Christians only, or simply Christians. Which leads us to our final section in this chapter.

Slogans Emphasizing Christ Alone and the Name "Christian"

The most famous of the Christocentric slogans, is *"No creed but Christ."* This phrase was originally part of the "No book but the Bible, no creed but Christ, no name but the divine" (with, occasionally, "no law but love" added). Those urging a restoration of the New Testament church in structure and spirit believed that the myriad of creeds that had sprung up since the days of first-century Christianity had divided believers rather than uniting them. While creeds (from the Latin *credo*, "I believe") were summations of Christian belief, sometimes these creeds took on a life of their own and were even used as a test of fellowship to exclude or debar other Christians.

Barton W. Stone accepted the Westminster Confession but with this reservation: "as far as I see it consistent with the word of God." Others rejected creeds outright. Alexander Campbell, while recognizing some truth in some creeds, deemed them "necessarily heretical and schismatical." In his debate with Nathan Rice he listed 13 reasons why creeds should not be a term of communion. Among them, their affront to Christ's supreme authority, their discouragement of deeper inquiry into scriptural truth, and their tendency to be "superfluous and redundant" (Paul M. Blowers, *The Encyclopedia of the Stone-Campbell Movement,* 2004). Regarding the latter, some said that if a creed said the *same thing* as Christ or the Bible, why say it at all? If a creed said *more* than Christ or the Bible said, it was saying too much. If a creed said *less* than what Christ or the Bible demanded, it was insufficient. And so came the clarion cry, "No creed but Christ!"

Walter Scott believed that the Good Confession made by Peter was the "golden oracle" of Scripture. "Thou art the Christ, the Son of the living God" (Matt. 16:16, KJV). He said, "The truth of the Christian faith is that Jesus is the Christ." He compared this singular truth to "the sun to which all other Christian truths are planets in a spiritual solar system." Every truth in Scripture revolves around Jesus Christ. Jesus said, ". . . the Scriptures . . . testify of Me" (John 5:39). Our only creed is Christ. Our only confession is Christ. Our character should be modeled after Christ. Our conduct should be controlled by Christ.

I once heard Richard Rogers preach a message called, "Hills Worth Dying On." There are very few hills worth dying on. The hill millions of martyrs have been willing to climb and die on is the hill crowned by the cross of Christ. They died because they were confessors—men, women, and children who confessed, "Thou art the Christ, the Son of the living God!" Not much else is worth dying for.

"No name but the divine." This slogan was a plea for believers in Christ to take His name and wear His name above all other names. Some felt that the name Christian was "oracularly given," citing Isaiah 62:2, "You shall be called by a new name, which the mouth of the LORD will name." That new name, they believed, was "Christian." They cited Acts 11:26, "And the disciples were first called Christians in Antioch." Perhaps we could say that God *assigned* the name but the enemies of Christ *maligned* the name (James 2:7).

"Christian" is a uniting name. Denominational names tend to divide ("denominate" means "to give a name to"). Albert Barnes said, "These divisions should be merged into the holy name Christian." Henry Ward Beecher agreed: "Let me speak in the language of heaven and call you Christian." Martin Luther pleaded, "I pray you, leave my name alone. Do not call yourselves Lutherans, but Christians." Charles Spurgeon was emphatic: "I say of the Baptist name, let it perish, but let Christ's name last forever." John Wesley agreed with him: "I wish the name Methodist might never be mentioned again, but lost in eternal oblivion." John Calvin said, "Acknowledge no unity except in Christ." Sometimes I wonder, "Where are the great church leaders of today who will echo their clarion call to call ourselves Christians only?"

> "Acknowledge no unity except in Christ."

To cite Albert Barnes again: "(Christian) is the distinguishing name of all the redeemed. It is not that we belong to this or that denomination: it is not that our names are connected with high and illustrious ancestors . . . it is that they are *Christians*. This binds them all together—a name which rises above every other appellation; which unites in one the inhabitants of distant nations and tribes of men; which connects the extremes of society, and places them on a common level; and which is a bond to unite in one family all those who love the Lord Jesus, though dwelling in different climes, speaking different languages, engaged in different pursuits in life, and occupying distant graves at death." Wise words, those!

Christian is a name all can wear—should *want* to wear! But a quick check of the Yellow Pages reveals the stark truth. We still prefer human names; we rather like them; we cling to them in spite of the Name that is above all other names, the name divinely given for the followers of Christ, *Christianos*, Christian, "a follower of Christ." The slogan "No name but the divine" is still one that needs to be heard, respected, and applied.

"Christians only, but not the only Christians." Leroy Garrett suggests that this motto may have evolved from John Wesley, "who urged his followers in America not to call themselves Methodists but simply Christians." We are Christians only. Later, the slogan was expanded to say, "We are Christians only, but not the only Christians." This was an effort to remove any spirit of judgmentalism in the movement to be Christians only. They were not saying that they were the *only* Christians in the world, but that they were striving to be Christians *only*. Only God knows those who are truly His, those who have "named the name of Christ" (2 Tim. 2:19).

An old story illustrates the truth of this slogan. George Whitefield once gave this illustration in a sermon delivered from the courthouse balcony in Philadelphia, Pennsylvania. He asked, "Father Abraham, whom have you in heaven? Any Episcopalians?"

"*No!*"

"Any Presbyterians?"

"*No!*"

"Have you any Independents or Seceders?"

"*No!*"

"Have you any Methodists?"

"*No, no, no!*"

"Whom have you there?"

"*We don't know those names here! All who are here are Christians!*"

"Oh, is this the case? Then God help us to forget party names and to become Christians in deed and truth."

> A Christian is all I am and all I ever wanted to be.
> A Christian is all everyone should be and ever want to be.
> Together in Christ let us be Christians and Christians only!

Chapter Six

THE BODY THAT WILLED TO DIE
DOCUMENTS ADVOCATING UNITY

The Constitution of the United States and the Declaration of Independence are two of the most important documents in U.S. history. The primary meaning of "document" is "an original or official paper relied upon as the basis, proof, or support of something." This would certainly be true of the political documents mentioned above. A secondary meaning is "a writing conveying information." That would be true of the "documents" mentioned in this chapter.

One of the most famous documents in all of church history would be Martin Luther's "Ninety-five Theses" which he nailed to the door of the Castle Church in Wittenberg, Germany, on October 31, 1517. Basically it was a document criticizing the system of granting indulgences and challenging all comers to debate the issue. In 1521 the Council of Wörms (pronounced *Vurms*) ordered Luther to retract his published views. Luther boldly replied, "Unless I am convicted of error by the testimony of Scripture, or by manifest reasoning, I stand convicted by the Scriptures to which I have appealed, and my conscience is taken captive by God's Word, I cannot and will not recant anything. For to act against our conscience is neither safe for us, nor open to us. On this I take my stand. I can do no other. God help me. Amen."

> "Unless I am convicted of error by the testimony of Scripture I cannot and will not recant anything."

Throughout the years men have sought to articulate their convictions by writing brief papers on particular subjects that were of great concern to them. These documents were more than short slogans yet less than full-length treatises. I do not believe the writers intended them to be "official" papers because they were often challenging "official" positions taken by others. The creators of these documents, like Luther, made their appeal to the highest authority, Holy Scripture.

The subtitle to C.A. Young's book *Historical Documents Advocating Christian Unity* (reprinted by College Press, 1985) reads as follows: "Epoch-making statements by leaders among the Disciples of Christ for the restoration of the Christianity of the New Testament—its doctrines, its ordinances, and its fruits." Young, at the time (1904), was managing editor of *The Christian Century.* Two of the "historical documents" (what we might call "position papers" today) contained in his book will be considered in this chapter: Barton W. Stone's "Last Will and Testament of the Springfield Presbytery" and Thomas Campbell's "Declaration and Address."

LAST WILL AND TESTAMENT OF THE SPRINGFIELD PRESBYTERY

The "Last Will and Testament of the Springfield Presbytery," published in 1804, has been called one of the first statements of religious freedom ever proclaimed in the Western Hemisphere. It was primarily the work of Barton W. Stone, a Presbyterian minister, present at one of the most famous camp meetings in American history, the storied Cane Ridge Revival of 1801. Following the revival, Stone and some other ministers formed the Springfield Presbytery in Bourbon County, Kentucky. But after realizing that Scripture no more supported a presbytery than it did a creed, they decided to disband the new organization. Stone and six other fellow ministers wrote and released the "Last Will and Testament of the Springfield Presbytery" F.D. Kershner has said, "The document is delightfully ironical and is one of the most brilliant written productions in theological literature."

"**We will, that this body die, be dissolved, and sink into union with the Body of Christ at large.**"

"Last Will" begins with an *imprimis* ("in the first place"): "We *will*, that this body die, be dissolved, and sink into union with the Body of Christ at large; for there is but one Body, and one Spirit, even as we are called in one hope of our calling."

Eleven "items" follow, a few of which are:

♦ "We *will*, that our name of distinction, with its *Reverend* title, be forgotten, that there be but one Lord over God's heritage, and his name One."

- "We *will*, that our power of making laws for the government of the church, and executing them by delegated authority, forever cease: that the people may have free course to the Bible, and adopt *the law of the Spirit of life in Christ Jesus.*"
- "We *will*, that the people henceforth take the Bible as the only sure guide to heaven; and as many as are offended with other books, which stand in competition with it, may cast them into the fire if they choose; for it is better to enter into life having one book, than having many to be cast into hell."
- "We *will*, that preachers and people, cultivate a spirit of mutual forbearance; pray more and dispute less; and while they behold the signs of the times, look up, and confidently expect that redemption draweth nigh."
- "Finally we *will*, that all our *sister bodies* read their Bibles carefully, that they may see their fate there determined, and prepare for death before it is too late."

> "We will, that preachers and people . . . pray more and dispute less."

"Last Will and Testament of the Springfield Presbytery" was signed by Barton W. Stone and five other witnesses on June 28, 1804. The irenic document closes with "The Witnesses' Address" which, in part, stated, "Let all Christians join with us, in crying to God day and night, to remove the obstacles which stand in the way of his work, and give him no rest till he make Jerusalem a praise in the earth. We heartily unite with our Christian brethren of every name, in thanksgiving to God for the display of his goodness in the glorious work he is carrying on in our Western country, which we hope will terminate in the universal spread of the gospel, and the unity of the church."

The framers of "Last Will" knew something that perhaps we have forgotten. "Unless a grain of wheat falls into the earth and dies, it remains by itself alone; but if it dies, it bears much fruit" (John 12:24, NASB). The "death" of the Springfield Presbytery that Stone and his fellow ministers willed and carried out was for the greater good of the kingdom of God. They were willing to lay aside their distinctive name—even wishing that they be forgotten altogether—in order to sink into union with the larger Body of Christ.

One of the greatest barriers to Christian unity today is the unwillingness of ecclesiastical bodies (denominations if you will) to "die and sink into union with the Body of Christ at large." The will to live, of course, is a stronger desire than the will to die. Push my head under the water and I will fight with fury to break the surface and breathe God's good air. No one wants to die. I look back on those plucky Presbyterians of 1804 and marvel at their audacity—and applaud their bravery. But who among us would be willing to do the same today? Are we too married to our "names of distinction" and too enraptured with our "powers of making laws for the government of the church"? We are like little individual kernels of wheat frantically fighting to stay on top of the soil where we can be seen and heard. We seem to have no interest in sinking into the soil, dying, and bearing much fruit by rising as the united Body of Christ, resulting in the "universal spread of the gospel."

> We are like little individual kernels of wheat frantically fighting to stay on top of the soil where we can be seen and heard.

Having the name "Christian" on your church building, however, doesn't necessarily mean that all who meet in that building are Christians in attitude and actions. Indeed, some churches probably need to remove the word "Christian" from their building or sign because of their sectarian spirit. Let us all be so filled with Christ that the first thing an unbiased observer would say is, "That person is a Christian!" Wouldn't it be wonderful if the unselfish spirit of Springfield would spread to all our churches today?

DECLARATION AND ADDRESS

Five years after the writing of "Last Will," another document was released. It was called the "Declaration and Address," written by Thomas Campbell and published in 1809 in Washington, Pennsylvania. Campbell came to America from Ireland where he had served as an ordained minister in the Seceder Presbyterian Church of Scotland

Documents

and North Ireland. He was serving as a missionary of the United Presbyterian Church (the American name for the Scotch-Irish Church) when he developed his convictions that Christianity should be undenominational in nature.

"Declaration and Address" contained thirteen basic propositions for achieving Christian unity. Frederick D. Kershner called it "one of the great classics in Christian literature." The depth of Campbell's conviction on the sin of division and the need for unity is seen in some sentences he wrote before launching into his proposals. Knofel Staton has paraphrased them as follows:

"Ministers and members alike, listen! There are no divisions either in the grave or in that world just beyond the grave. *There* our divisions will come to an end. *There* Christians *will* unite! So I pray to God that we can find it in our hearts to put an end to our short-lived divisions *here.* And if we do, we will leave a tremendous blessing behind us. Wouldn't you like to leave a united Church when you die? What a joy that would be!" (*The Paraphrase of Thomas Campbell's* **Declaration and Address** *by Knofel Staton*).

> "There are no divisions either in the grave or in that world just beyond the grave. *There* our divisions will come to an end. *There* Christians will unite!"

Staton's modern paraphrase of Campbell's thirteen propositions for unity is as follows:

- The Church of Christ on earth is indispensably, intentionally, and structurally one. It includes *everyone* in *any* place who professes trust and obedience to Christ in all matters according to the Scriptures; and who demonstrates such in character and conduct. No one else can be called a Christian.

- Although the Church of Christ on earth exists in different locations, there should be no divisions among congregations. Each congregation should receive the other as Christ Jesus has. That would manifest God's character before all. To facilitate this, all congregations should observe the same practices and speak the same principles.

- In order to carry this out, nothing should be forced upon Christians except what is clearly taught in the Word of God.

> **Nothing should be forced upon Christians except what is clearly taught in the Word of God.**

Nothing should be treated in the constitution and by-laws as divine authority unless it is clearly taught in the Word of God. Thus human traditions, regardless of "how long we've done it that way," cannot be our authority.

- Although God's revealed will is expressed in both the Old and New Testament books, the New Testament books contain the immediate constitution for the worship, discipline, and government of the corporate church and for the duties of the individual members.

- Nothing ought to be received into the beliefs and worship of the Church nor made the test of fellowship which is not as old as the New Testament books.

  No one should dictate binding directives outlining exactly *how* procedures have to be carried out if the New Testament is silent about such procedures. It is enough if we fulfill the intent of those practices where procedures are not clearly spelled out.

- The "conclusions" we arrive at from systematic Scriptural study, as doctrinally valid and valuable as they may be, should not be used as tests of fellowship. "Conclusions" result from our reasoning endeavors. But a man's faith must stand upon the power and truth of God, not in the wisdom of men. Our "conclusions" should be used for building up those who are already Christians, not for admittance exams to those who are not.

- Our "conclusions" will certainly vary as we systematically study the many various topics within Christianity. The more comprehensibly we study and communicate a topic, the better. However, let us realize that the Church is made up of all levels of spiritual maturity—and understanding—spiritual babes, spiritual adolescents, spiritual young adults, spiritual adults (figuratively speaking). That means we will always have differences in our understandings and thus in our conclusions. But these differences should not be used as tests of fellowship.

Documents

- It is not necessary that people see *all* God's truth exactly alike before they are added to His Church. What is necessary it that they recognize two things: (1) their lost condition and (2) Jesus' way of salvation. And then declare their faith in Him and their willingness to obey Him in all things.

> It is not necessary that people see all God's truth exactly alike before they are added to His Church.

- Anyone who has made such a declaration should consider anyone else who has made such an acknowledgement as saints of God and should love such as brothers. For such people are children of the same family, temples of the same Spirit, members of the same body, subjects of the same grace, objects of the same Divine love, bought with the same price, and joint-heirs of the same inheritance. And whom God hath joined together no man should dare to put aside.

- Division among Christians is a repulsive evil filled with many tragedies. Here are three of those tragedies: (1) It is *anti-Christian*, because it destroys the visible unity of the body of Christ. Division suggests that Christ is divided against Himself by excluding and excommunicating a part of Himself. (2) It is *antiscriptural*, because it is strictly forbidden by God. (3) It is *antinatural,* because it motivates Christians to hate and oppose one another who are commanded by God to love one another as brothers. In summary, divisions are a product of and produce confusion and every evil work.

- All the past and present corruptions and divisions in the Church have resulted from two causes: (1) The partial neglect of the clearly expressed will of God; (2) the insistence that human opinions and hobby horses be accepted in the belief, life, and worship of the Church.

- There are four practices necessary if the Church is to manifest the maturity and manners God wants: (1) That no one be admitted who does not acknowledge faith in Christ and obedience to Him. (2) That no one be kept who doesn't back up that acknowledgement with character and conduct. (3) That properly qualified preachers teach nothing other than what is clearly expressed in the Word of God. (4) That those preachers observe all the Divine ordinances which the Church in the New Testament books observed—in the way that the Church observed them.

- That any additions to the New Testament program which circumstances may seem to require, shall be regarded as human expedients and shall not be given a place of higher authority in the church than is permitted by the fallible character of their origin. (This thirteenth and final proposition is a paraphrase written by Frederick D. Kershner. Another summary, by Douglas A. Foster, reads, "Matters of 'expedience' in the execution of the divine ordinances must be identified as such and acted on without becoming objects of contention.")

"Declaration and Address" closes with a heartfelt appeal for all believers in Christ to associate with one another, continue to study Scripture, and unite in Christ. Citing John 13:34,35 and John 17:20,21, Campbell concluded, "Let us leave this Babel of confusion. Let us lean upon Christ, embrace each other in Him while holding fast the unity of the Spirit in the bond of peace. Our unity with one another is the best observable evidence of our union with Christ. . . . May the Lord hasten it in His time" (*The Paraphrase of Thomas Campbell's Declaration and Address* by Knofel Staton).

Barton W. Stone, Thomas Campbell, and others who desired to answer Christ's prayer for unity did more than just preach about and write about it. At a New Year's Day gathering in Lexington, Kentucky, in 1832, many unity-minded brethren came together in a great union service. Stone and "Racoon" John Smith, a former Baptist, were chosen to speak but were given instructions to "avoid the spirit and manner of controversy, and give their plans of union freely, but without reference to party distinctions." Smith spoke first. "God has but one people on the earth. He has given to them but one Book, and therein exhorts and com-

"While there is but one faith, there may be ten thousand opinions; and hence, if Christians are ever to be one, they must be one in faith, and not in opinion."

mands them to be one family. . . . The prayer of the Savior, and the whole tenor of his teaching, clearly shows that it is God's will that his children should be united. . . . While there is but one faith, there may be ten thousand opinions; and hence, if Christians are ever to be one, they must be one in faith, and not in opinion . . . Let us then, my brethren, be no longer Campbellites or Stoneites, or New Lights or Old Lights, or any other kind of lights, but let us all come to the Bible, and to the Bible alone, as the only book in the world that can give us all the Light we need."

Stone arose and said, "I have not one objection to the ground laid down by him as the true scriptural basis of union among the people of God; and I am willing to give him, here and now, my hand." He then turned to Smith and offered him his hand, "a hand trembling with rapture and brotherly love, and it was grasped by a hand full of honest pledges of fellowship, and the union was virtually accomplished." Across the aisles, Christians grasped the hands of brothers and sisters and spontaneously broke into song. "On the Lord's Day, they broke the loaf together, and in that sweet and solemn communion, again pledged to each other their brotherly love" (*Life of Elder John Smith*, John Augustus Williams, Gospel Advocate Co., 1956 as cited in *Union on the King's Highway,* Dean Mills, College Press, 1987).

"Behold, how good and pleasant it is for brethren to dwell together in unity!" (Ps. 133:1).

These two documents, produced only a few short years apart, written by sincere men whose dedicated followers would take their words to heart and unite on the premises proffered by both men, were in perfect agreement on at least seven principles, namely:

♦ Scripture is the only sure rule of faith and practice for the church.
♦ Inferences and opinions should never be made tests of fellowship.
♦ The church is one—there is but one Body.
♦ Christians should maintain the unity of the Spirit in the bond of peace.
♦ The name of Christ is to be preferred above all human names.

Documents

- ♦ A divided Christendom shames Christ and is a horrible witness.
- ♦ Christian unity is absolutely essential to the salvation of the world.

Breathes there a soul reading these words that could not say "Amen!" to these biblical principles?

Breathes there a soul who is willing to say, "I am willing to give, here and now my hand"?

Some 200 years later I hear the whispers of these irenic souls:

> *"Let all Christians join with us, in crying to God day and night, to remove the obstacles which stand in the way of his work, and give him no rest till he make Jerusalem a praise in the earth!"*

> *"Oh! That ministers and people would but consider, that there are no divisions in the grave; nor in that world which lies beyond it: there our divisions must come to an end. We must all unite here. Would to God we could find it in our hearts to put an end to our short-loved divisions here, that so we might leave a blessing behind us, even a happy and united church!"*

Together in Christ we can:

Join with them in a similar spirit,
Do our part to bring an end to division,
Leave a blessing behind us, a happy and united church!

Chapter Seven

MAY I SAY SOMETHING?
STATEMENTS ON UNITY
(PART I)

The following statements on unity do not come from "official" spokesmen. They are selected statements on unity that were made by those who have acted like "statesmen" in the noble quest for Christian unity. I asked about one hundred friends and associates for their help in compiling a list of good quotations, and these are the ones that made the final cut. Some of the statements are from the past and others are from those living in the present. Hopefully all of these statesmanlike statements will steer us on a better course for the future as we seek to be "together in Christ." I wanted to list these quotes according to subject matter but there was so much overlap in some of the statements that I finally decided just to list them alphabetically according to the statesman's last name. These are for the most part quotes without comment. Some of these statesmen, having gone on to that better land, are still "speaking." The rest remain to carry on their righteous work to "make every effort to keep the unity of the Spirit in the bond of peace."

Allen, C. Ermal
"A divided church is powerless to present the Gospel of Christ effectively to a lost and dying world. Jesus prayed for unity, just as the apostles of Christ commanded it, because unity is necessary 'that the world may believe' (John 17:21). Therefore, before we start or take up a dispute in the church, we must ask, 'How will this affect our ability to preach Christ and him crucified? Is the loss of a credible witness to the love of God really worth winning this fight?'"

Allen, C. Leonard
"The most pressing question facing Churches of Christ today is the question, Can we recover 'the word of the cross' in its biblical fullness? No other question even comes close to this one."

Allen, F.G.

"To deny that there are Christians apart from those who stand identified with us in our work would make our plea for Christian union both meaningless and senseless. While we believe many identified with the denominations are Christians, they have taken on much that is neither Christianity nor any part of it; and this we labor to have them put away. . . . It will be seen, therefore, that while we claim to be Christians only, we do not claim to be the only Christians. Our principles will not allow us to be anything else. . . ."

Anderson, Lynn

"We have been separated far too long over far too little."

"Our common mission is still the Great Commission."

"It is high time for each of us to leave behind our self-perceptions of superiority and whatever deep wounds we may have received in the past. Let us stand together eagerly at the place of level ground—the foot of the cross."

> "We have been separated far too long over far too little."

Armour, Mike

"Sectarian people overlook the lesson from the church in Sardis, a congregation variously described by Jesus as asleep and dead. Yet He noted that some in Sardis had not soiled their garments. 'They will walk with me in white,' He promised, saying in effect *that people can go to heaven from a church bound for perdition.*"

"The bottom line is, 'Are we of Christ?' If so, then we must find ways to surmount the barriers that time, habit and ego have raised between us."

Armstrong, J.N.

"The thing that is now causing trouble is this divisive spirit, this self-righteous, dogmatic, intolerant spirit, that made a determined effort to divide an otherwise united brotherhood. . . . As a result some have 'lined up,' some 'shut up,' and others suffered martyrdom for their convictions."

> "It's not our differences that hurt, but our manner of differing."

"It's not our differences that hurt, but our manner of differing."

Atchley, Rick

"For a hundred years we have served God apart . . . only God knows what we can do in the next hundred years serving Him together. But I know this—I know it will be more than we could ask or imagine."

Beam, Ernest

"Brethren, we here this day need not to *establish* unity. We need but to recognize it is ours of right by the making of the Lord."

"Like editor John F. Rowe, who was ever for worship without the assistance of an instrument, I too, say, 'Strike, but hear me: By the grace of God, I am determined not to be held responsible for the division and alienation of God's people by fighting over an organ!'"

Blakely, Fred O.

"The way to the unity that is in Christ is for everyone concerned to get into Him, and 'grow up into Him in all things' (Eph. 4:15). That is the formula for 'the unity of the Spirit' and 'of the faith' prescribed by Paul in the context of that passage, as it is the premise of all new-covenant writings that speak to that subject."

Blakely, Given O.

"The type of unity that exists between the Father and the Son is the only kind of unity that is acceptable among believers—'as We are one!'"

"Unanimity among brethren cannot possibly require more effort than being in fellowship with the Lord and His Christ!"

"Is it possible that more is required to unite men with one another than to unite them with the Living God? The day that unity among men in Christ requires more than unity between God and men is the day men have usurped the throne of the universe!"

> "Is it possible that more is required to unite men with one another than to unite them with the Living God?"

"The unity of those who believe on Christ is the catalyst for the conversion of the world! If those that have named the name of the Lord do not love and prefer one another, how will the world be convinced God loves them?"

Boles, Kenny

"Unity is imperative because it's what Jesus prayed for. 'May they be brought to complete unity' (John 17:23). It was the night before He died—this was His final wish! Even now my mother is dying of cancer. What kind of a son would ignore her wishes? What kind of a person would ignore Christ's dying wish?"

Boll, R.H.

"That differences of views and doctrines should exist in the church of the Lord is not strange. Nor is it in itself bad. When free brethren study God's word independently it is to be expected that on one point and another they will arrive at different conclusions. Where brotherly love rules, these different views and the discussions that follow are mutually helpful. Where motives other than love control, differences result in dissension, strife, bitterness, sectarian parties and partisan hate. The blame in such a case, however, does not rest on the differences themselves, but on the spirit and attitude of those who differ. The wrong comes in when lines are drawn, when brethren are branded, ostracized, disfellowshipped."

Boultinghouse, Denny

"We must take great care . . . that we not bind people to a creed, written or unwritten. Affirming Christ as our only creed will work wonders in helping us to be the New Testament church we so desperately want to be. Obviously anyone who affirms Jesus will always be submissive to his words. Thus our loyalty will be to the Christ of Scripture and not to any man-made creed. That is a plea worth pursuing."

Bream, Jr., Harvey C.

"Jesus' appeal was not to personality, logic or programs. It was to the word of God. If we are to win people to Jesus Christ, that must be our appeal too. The issue is not basically one of faith or repentance or baptism, or any other doctrine. The issue is authority. . . . We need to honor our Lord's prayer for those who would believe in Him through the apostles' word. We do this by faithfully teaching and preaching the authoritative word of God in its fullness."

Brewer, G.C.

"Nothing should separate us from each other unless it is something that separates us from God."

"Nothing should separate us from each other unless it is something that separates us from God."

Butterworth, V.E.

"Only in the cross of Christ can there be unity."

Campbell, Alexander

"The only apostolic and divine confession of faith which God, the Father of all, has laid for the church—and that on which Jesus himself said he would build it, is the sublime and supreme proposition: THAT JESUS OF NAZARETH IS THE MESSIAH, THE SON OF THE LIVING GOD. This is the peculiarity of the Christian system: its specific attribute."

"The Christian religion is a *personal* concern. It is confidence in a person, love to a person, delight in a person—not confidence in a doctrine or love to a party. Jesus Christ is the object on which the Christian's faith, hope and love terminate."

"So long as any man, woman or child declares his confidence in Jesus of Nazareth as God's own Son, that He was delivered for our offenses, and raised again for our justification; or, in other words, that Jesus is the Messiah, the Savior of men; and so long as he exhibits a willingness to obey Him in all things according to his knowledge, so long will I receive him as a Christian brother and treat him as such."

"Let the Bible be substituted for all human creeds; facts, for definitions; things, for words; faith, for speculation; unity of faith, for unity of opinion; the positive commands of God, for human legislation and tradition; piety, for ceremony; morality, for partisan zeal; the practice of religion, for the profession of it,—and the work is done."

Campbell, Thomas

". . . the Church of Christ upon earth is essentially, intentionally, and constitutionally one, consisting of all those in every place that profess their faith in Christ and obedience to Him in all things according to the scriptures, and that manifest the same by their tempers and conduct, and of none else, as none else can be truly and properly called Christians."

"Our desire, therefore, for ourselves and our brethren would be, that, rejecting human opinions and the inventions of men as of any authority, or as having any place in the Church of God, we might forever cease from farther contentions about such things; returning to, and holding fast by, the original standard; taking the divine word alone for our rule; the Holy Spirit for our teacher and guide, to lead us into all truth; and Christ alone, as exhibited in the word, for our salvation, that, by so doing, we may be at peace among ourselves, follow peace with all men, and holiness, without which no man shall see the Lord."

". . . although inferences and deductions from scripture premises, when fairly inferred, may be truly called the doctrines of God's holy word, yet are they not formally binding upon the consciences of Christians farther than they perceive the connection, and evidently see that they are so; for their faith must not stand in the wisdom of men, but in the power and veracity of God."

"Until you associate, consult, and advise together, and in a friendly manner explore the subject, nothing can be done."

"If you will show me how your inquiry affects in any way your eternal salvation I will endeavor to answer your question." (When asked how to determine what is essential.)

Chambers, Bob

"A unity which helps to 'make disciples of all the nations' has Heaven's approval. A unity which hinders the execution of our Lord's final instructions has Heaven's anathema."

Clark, N.L.

"Had child-like faith and true brotherly love, tempered with reason and moderation, guided professed followers of Christ in past centuries, we should never have had our denominational bodies or the existing divisions among those who call themselves simply disciples of Christ."

DeWelt, Chris

"When our heart-focus is upon the Father, then division moves to the back burner—or clear off the stove!"

"To the degree that the people of God go to the Throne on their own and see Him there, to that degree we are made one."

"Prayer is where it begins. Prayer is where it happens. On its knees, God's kingdom can conquer the hearts of men."

"Once we recognize brotherhood, it is incumbent upon us to assume the responsibilities of family!"

"Not only have we not recognized the flock of God, we have butchered His sheep!"

"It really seems simple. Take the message of salvation to every person on earth. They deserve the chance to hear it at least one time before they die. Is that so hard? Can we not come together and get the job done?"

DeWelt, Don

"Our Lord said, 'Blessed are the peacemakers for they shall be called the children of God.' The only begotten child of God was the first peacemaker—and he was crucified! Such has been the experience of many since."

"Some day I'm going to write a book and call it *Agree with Me or Go to Hell!* But then I realized Someone has already written that Book!"

"If we wait until we are certain all of our brothers agree with us, we shall wait one long time! Suppose the Father waited until we all agreed with Him before He invited us? We never would have a feast!"

"It is not necessary for me to agree with you nor you to agree with me to be right or understand the truth. The word of God is truth. The word is right, not what we understand about it."

> "If we wait until we are certain all of our brothers agree with us, we shall wait one long time!"

"We can't do everything, but we can do something. We can't put the whole splintered brotherhood back together again, but we can reach out to take at least one hand and say, 'Brother, do you suppose we could do this work for the Lord . . . together?"

"In one sense Christ's prayer has already been answered: all who believe on his name are members of the same body."

"One day the scales of sectarianism will drop from our eyes and we will accept each other as God in Christ accepts us!"

Errett, Isaac

"If a people pleading for the union of all Christians cannot maintain the unity of the Spirit in the bond of peace in their own limited communion, and peaceably dispose of all such questions as are mentioned above [instrumental music in worship and a developing pastor system], and a great many more, then is this plea for union as ridiculous a farce as was ever played before the public. The Apostolic churches had much graver errors in doctrine and practice to dispose of than any that are troubling us. . . . The lessons of Christian liberty, of tolerance and forbearance, of patience and gentleness taught by the apostles, need to be carefully attended to. . . . As long as we are one in the faith of Christ and in acknowledging the supremacy of His authority, we will remain one people; and free and kindly discussion will bring us out of our differences."

"It is possible to do nothing directly to cause division, and yet to sin against the church and against Christ by causing offense. It is possible to abuse and pervert the very reasons that are urged against division in such a way as to cause those stumblings. If one class is warned against causing division, the other is warned with equal earnestness against causing offenses. Those are alike sins against the integrity of the body of Christ."

"All who trust in the Son of God and obey Him, are our brethren, however wrong they may be about anything else; and those who do not trust in this Divine Savior for salvation and obey His commandments, are not our brethren, however intelligent and excellent they many be. . . ."

> "All who trust in the Son of God and obey Him, are our brethren, however wrong they may be about anything else."

"If men are right about Christ, Christ will bring them right about everything else."

Faull, George L.

"In what God has revealed, let us have unity. In what He has not revealed, let us have liberty. In innovations, let us have caution not to violate another's conscience. In all things, let us have love, which means seeking the other man's good."

"Let us determine to have the same Head (Lord), be in the one Body, led by the same Spirit, serving the same Lord, immersed into one Body, giving us the same hope; then and only then do we have any hope of seeing the same God."

Ferguson, Everett

"There is room for a diversity that seeks unity; there is no place for a diversity born of party spirit."

"Blest be the tie that binds our hearts in Christian love and our hands in Christian service."

"The cross and baptism are the basis of Christian unity (1 Cor. 1:13)."

"In Romans 12 and 1 Corinthians 12 unity unfolds in diversity; the situation is not diversity coming together in unity."

Fife, Robert O.

"Only that which is viable in a concentration camp should be considered essential to a believer's life in Christ, or essential to the existence of the Church."

"Because we may not in everything see eye to eye, can we not in anything work shoulder to shoulder? Does fellowship in anything constitute approval of everything?"

"Christian unity is not only a gift to be kept, it is also a goal to be attained."

Fitch, Alger

"Unity based upon a lie would never please the God of truth."

"Some things are worse than division. A union maintained by the loss of liberty is not the Christian ideal."

> "Unity based upon a lie would never please the God of truth."

"What denominational merger, in the century now passing, has resulted in an upsurge in evangelistic thrust?"

"A unity based on any single creedal statement or a combination of many will only result in unity among those whose consciences accept that creed and separation from those who do not."

Foster, Douglas A.

"The Scriptures are quite plain about the essential foundation for correct beliefs and practices—humility, mercy, gentleness, love of peace, and forbearance. . . . It is absolutely essential to realize that without these things, without the mind and attitude of Christ, there can be no correct belief or practice."

"Restoration of correct doctrine is not the end. True restoration must result in a life characterized by a proper relationship to Christ; a life distinguished by Christ's humility, his love, his righteousness and his selfless concern for others. This . . . is God's prescription for unity."

"We have missed what Christianity and Christian doctrine is all about—reconciliation. When in grappling to understand and articulate specific doctrines we come together in love with other believers, assuming both the sincerity and imperfection of all parties, we will have *begun* to see the face of unity."

Foster, R.C.

"No human being can claim a copyright on all truth. We must always be ready to hold the Scripture, and not ourselves, as the divine pattern. The proposition of restoring the church as seen in the New Testament resolves itself into these declarations: If anything that I believe or practice is not in accord with the New Testament, then I desire to discover it and abandon it. If anything the New Testament teaches is missing from my belief or practice, then I want to include it. Speak, Lord; for thy servant heareth."

Fowler, Harold

"It is pretty hard to keep kicking a dog that keeps licking your hand. And by the grace of God, I for one am determined to be that dog. . . . So often I have found beneath that seemingly forbidding exterior, a Christian to love, and in loving him, found a brother."

Fudge, Edward

"The point is not who said it first, but where they got it. If it came from God, it's for all his people."

"My Christian identity is not defined by denominational membership—even in a nondenominational denomination. To clarify my own identity, it is simply and solely 'to be found in Christ, not having a righteousness of my own . . . but that which is through faith in Christ, the righteousness which is from God by faith' (Phil.3:9)."

"The point is not who said it first, but where they got it. If it came from God, it's for all his people."

"We do not disrespect the past by looking to the future, or by living in the present. We are not responsible for our ancestors, but rather for our children."

Garfield, James A.

"We plead for the union of God's people on the Bible and the Bible alone."

Garrett, Leroy

"It should impress us profoundly that our Lord, even in his last hours, should pray for the oneness of his disciples. That alone should make divisions among Christians intolerable. And should it not also lead us to pray for the unity of all God's peoples, including in our assemblies?"

"Ecumenical gatherings and unity forums have their place, but unity in Christ is not realized by human ingenuity, however well-intentioned. It is a gift of the Spirit—'preserve the Spirit's unity in the bond of peace' (Eph. 4:3)."

"Christian unity and evangelism are interrelated. Jesus made this strikingly clear in his prayer for unity, even implying that a divided church cannot effectively evangelize. The church is to be *one* so the world can be *won*."

"The fewer essentials, the broader the unity; the more essentials required, the narrower the circle of unity."

"We can never unite on opinions. We can unite only on the basic truth of the gospel, allowing for opinions as private property—and not imposed on others."

Goad, Steven Clark

"Aren't we brothers and sisters in Christ because of what He did at Calvary, not because of what we might do or say on any given Sunday?"

Hardeman, N.B.

"I have never been so egotistic as to say that my brethren with whom I commune on the first day of the week are the ONLY Christians on this earth. I never said that in my life. I do make the claim that we are Christians ONLY. But there is a vast difference between that expression and the one formerly made. . . ."

Hawley, Monroe

"When correct doctrine becomes the focus of our faith, what one believes assumes greater importance than the person in whom one believes. The basis of divine acceptance then becomes a set of ideas rather than the consecrated life of the believer."

> "One cannot preach Christ without preaching the Bible, but it is possible to preach from the Bible without preaching Christ."

"One cannot preach Christ without preaching the Bible, but it is possible to preach from the Bible without preaching Christ."

"Unless our faith focuses on Jesus there is no way we can completely restore apostolic Christianity."

Hicks, Olan

"God's laws are not written between the lines of the Bible. They are written on the lines of the Bible. These will stand in eternity. But human deductions are all destined to 'perish with the using, after the doctrines and commandments of men.' In the meantime, may they not be allowed to divide us any longer."

Humble, Bill J.

"The dream of a living restoration is that people anywhere can search the Scripture, rediscover and obey its teaching, and then be added to the body of Christ. The seed of the kingdom can be planted anywhere."

"Our sense of fellowship in the church needs to be focused on the family and not on issues, for only then will our fragile fellowship be transformed into loving concern that God intended for his children to have for one another."

Hunt, Donald G.

"'Love the brotherhood.' Then, there is a divine brotherhood. Who are in that brotherhood? All who are sons of God are naturally brothers of one another. Therefore, the true brotherhood, the only brotherhood that God has anything to do with, is the brotherhood of those who are spiritually born into His family."

Idleman, Ken

"There are four pillars on which the church must stand. We must rally as one around these four absolutes: the Lordship of Christ, the authority of the Bible, the unity of believers, the evangelization of the world."

"New Testament Christianity need not be popularly embraced to be validated, but it is especially encouraging when it is recognized for what it is—light for our age."

Jacobs, Lyndsay

"We cannot preach reconciliation and practice assassination."

Jessup, Bryce

"If we belong to Christ, we are already united as members of His Body; our task is learning how to express it in relationships so that Jesus is seen as the only credible and incredible Savior of the world."

> "Family unity is not outdated. It is mandated."

"Family unity is not outdated. It is mandated."

Jessup, William L.

"And I believe, Christian friends, there isn't *any* problem that two Christian people can have—who possess the mind of Christ and the spirit of Christ—there isn't *any* problem but what those two can solve at the feet of Jesus Christ!" (His last words, literally. He died right after closing his sermon with these words in an evening service at Morgan Hill, California.)

> What a way to go!
> Urging Christians to solve their differences at the foot of the cross!
> Together in Christ let us go and do likewise!

Chapter Eight

MAY I SAY SOMETHING?
STATEMENTS ON UNITY
(PART II)

Kearley, Furman

"Whomever God has received, I must receive. Whomever Christ has received, I must receive. God's child is my brother. Christ's brother is my brother. Understanding and properly applying this principle will go a long way toward healing division and creating unity among God's people."

"We must make everything a test of fellowship which God, Christ, the Holy Spirit, and the holy scriptures make a test of fellowship. Christian fellowship is not wide open with no limitations . . . .On the other hand, as clearly taught in Romans 14, we must make nothing a test of fellowship which God, Christ, the Holy Spirit, and the holy scriptures have not made a test of fellowship."

Ketcherside, W. Carl

"I shall make nothing a test of fellowship which God has not made a condition of salvation."

"I shall be a brother to all who have been begotten by my Father."

"Brotherhood based upon Fatherhood, fraternity based upon paternity, this shall be my standard because it is scriptural."

> "I shall make nothing a test of fellowship which God has not made a condition of salvation."

"I have no half-brothers or step-brothers in the Lord. I accept you where you are and as you are. If you are good enough to be his son or daughter you are not too bad to be my brother or sister."

"If a man is good enough for God to receive he is not too bad for me to accept."

"The unity of the Spirit is one of community, not conformity; of diversity, not uniformity."

> "If a man is good enough for God to receive he is not too bad for me to accept."

"Our peace is a person, not a plan or a program."

"If fellowship in Christ was conditioned upon perfect agreement, there would be no place for forbearance, and the instruction to 'forbear one another in love' would be useless. Forbearance is never exercised toward those who see everything as you do."

"My only creed is Christ, and while I respect every rock of truth scattered over God's revelational landscape, I will build upon none of these."

"We are not one because we had the same experience in the flesh but because we are in One who experienced the same thing in the flesh for all of us."

"We are united not because of what we know, but because of Who we know."

"I have steadfastly set my face in the direction of the unity of all believers in Christ Jesus my Lord. I shall pray for it, plead for it, and proclaim it. I shall never be deterred. I shall never become discouraged. I will never be satisfied until all of us regard one another as God regards all of us. And when the time comes that the pen drops from my nerveless fingers, and my tongue cleaves to the roof of my mouth, I shall rest content, if on the gray marble above my head can be chiseled the words, 'He preached peace to them that are afar off and to them that are nigh!'"

Knowles, Dale V.

"Let the world not only hear us proclaim the unity of the Spirit in the bond of peace, but see it in our love for one another, as Jesus loves us."

Knutson, Jim

"We are not the sum of God's people, but we are some of God's people."

Lane, Tom

"We are each links in a chain of fellowship that connects all believers everywhere and forever. Unity means we recognize and practice brotherhood with Christians near and far. We acknowledge our common faith."

Langford, Thomas A.

"Nothing that divides us can be more important than the blood that was shed to make us one."

"Any title or church name that is used to designate only a part of the great family of God is too narrow."

"To deny fellowship to our brothers and sisters who trust and obey the Lord to the best of their understanding is to argue that we ourselves are perfect in heart and practice and therefore qualified to judge others by our perfect standard of conduct."

"Nothing that divides us can be more important than the blood that was shed to make us one."

"A priority concern for the lost would make some of the issues over which we have divided seem relatively less important."

"When I draw the lines of fellowship just outside the circle of those who agree with me, do I dare suggest that God's grace covers my sins and imperfections but not those whose study leads them to conclusions different from mine?"

"The essentials are necessary to our salvation. The post-baptismal differences, while not always comfortable, provide opportunities for mutual respect and study; they are not occasions for dividing the Body."

"How can any of us, moved by the Spirit, deny fellowship to a brother who also is host to the Spirit?"

Larimore, T.B.

"When Brother Campbell took my confession, on my twenty-first birthday, he questioned me relative to none of these 'matters now retarding the progress of the cause of Christ.' While thousands have stood before me, hand in mine, and made 'the good confession,' I have never questioned one of them about these 'matters.' Shall I now renounce and disfellowship all of these who do not understand these things exactly as I understand them? They may refuse to recognize or fellowship with me; but I will never refuse to recognize or fellowship or affiliate with them—never."

"May the Lord grant that I may die before I sow discord among brethren. I have never done so yet—never. I have never introduced, advocated, agitated, said, or done anything that could tend to dissever church, family, or friends. I love the sentiment of the son of America who said, 'If I have not the power to lift men to the skies, I thank my God that I have not the will to drag angels down . . . If I cannot bless, then let me not live. . . . "

"I prefer to sit on the issues and stand on Jesus Christ."

Lawson, Leroy

"The church belongs to Christ. We have no authority to change the teachings, rewrite the rules, alter membership requirements, or usurp his place. The church is not a democracy."

"Our message is that 'Jesus is the Christ, the Son of the living God.' We require no other creed. He alone is Lord and Savior."

Leggett, Marshall

"Christian is the most honorable name a person can wear. It contains and carries all that it means to belong to Christ. It represents those who have become children of God, with all the rights, privileges, and honors appertaining thereto."

"The restoration ideal and Christian unity will remain the means to a greater end—the evangelization of the world. But God's Word makes it crystal clear that the latter one depends upon the former two. Jesus prayed for unity that all men might believe."

Lemmons, Reuel

> "I had rather be the Roman soldier that thrust the sword into the body of my Lord than to be the man today who drives a wedge into the body of Christ."

"When brethren differ each is obligated to accept the possibility that he could be wrong—unless, of course, he thinks he is infallible. When groups of brethren differ they have the same obligation. A failure to accept this responsibility is really behind every division we have ever had."

"Unity at the expense of doctrine is unacceptable, and doctrine at the expense of doctrine is obnoxious."

"We cannot 'unbrother' what God has 'brothered.'"

"I had rather be the Roman soldier that thrust the sword into the body of my Lord than to be the man today who drives a wedge into the body of Christ."

Lipscomb, David

"The spirit that promotes unity and harmony among men comes from God. Unity and harmony of action are impossible in a way not provided by God. That unity is gained and maintained by doing the will of God. It requires no negotiations or arrangements among men to unite them as one in Christ. If we are in Christ, we cannot help being one with all who are in Christ."

"So long as a man really desires to do right, to serve the Lord, to obey His commands, we cannot withdraw from him. We are willing to accept him as a brother, no matter how ignorant he may be, or how far short of the perfect standard his life may fall from his ignorance. . . . We will maintain the truth, press the truth upon him, compromise not one word or iota of that truth, yet forbear with the ignorance, the weakness of our brother who is anxious, but not yet able to see the truth. . . . Why

> "How do I know that the line beyond which ignorance damns, is behind me, not before me?"

should I not, when I fall so far short of perfect knowledge myself? How do I know that the line beyond which ignorance damns, is behind me, not before me? If I have no forbearance with his ignorance, how can I expect God to forbear with mine? . . . So long then as a man exhibits a teachable disposition, is willing to hear, to learn and obey the truth of God, I care not how far he may be, how ignorant he is, I am willing to recognize him as a brother."

Lovell, Jimmy

"Every person born into the family of God is my brother and regardless of his personal opinion . . . if he came to the place where I worship and did not prove himself a problem by trying to push his opinions on others, he would be most welcome as far as I am concerned."

". . . I am just simple enough to believe that Jesus knew what he was talking about when he said, 'Except a man be born of water and the Spirit he cannot enter the kingdom of God' (John 3:5). There are untold thousands of persons around our world who have been born into the kingdom of God who may know no more about Christianity than those 3,000 baptized on Pentecost."

Statements

Lown, W.F.

"Though everyone has a right to his opinions, that does not entitle him to be ignorant of the facts."

Maddack, David

"The only way we are ever going to really have unity—the only way we are ever going to truly walk toward one hope—that way, is the way of Jesus. And the way of Jesus is the way of the cross. Crucifixion will be the means to our unity. We deny ourselves, we take up our cross, and we follow Jesus."

"Let this be our plea and our prayer for our brethren: What man has put asunder—may God join together!"

McGarvey, J. W.

"It was this supreme devotion to the word of God that developed a movement having at first only the union of believers in view, into one having in view the complete restoration of primitive Christianity in its faith, its ordinances and its life, with union as a necessary result. . . . It has made what we call our Reformation the mightiest instrument for the furtherance of Christian unity thus far known to history."

"I have never proposed to withdraw fellowship from brethren simply because of their use of instrumental music in the worship."

Mills, Dean

"When world evangelism once more becomes the primary goal of the brotherhood, the prayer of Jesus will again be taken seriously."

Mouton, Boyce

"There is a dramatic difference between the church that says, 'We are right,' and the church that says, 'He is right!'"

"Christian unity is not the result of 'conformation,' but 'transformation.'"

"If we cannot preach it everywhere, maybe we should not preach it anywhere."

"It is the eternal plan of God to call men out of a confused and divided world and unite them with Jesus Christ."

"When we die to self and become one with Christ, we lose our former identity. . . . This unity can be considered as spiritual synergy. It calls upon people from every kindred, nation, and tongue to deny themselves and be alloyed with Christ."

"Since Jesus is not ashamed of His imperfect brethren, we should not be ashamed of ours."

"Since Jesus is not ashamed of His imperfect brethren, we should not be ashamed of ours."

Murch, James DeForest

"The true unity of the Church derives, not from some centralized ecclesiastical structure, but from real spiritual substance."

"The testimony and challenge of this company of 'Christians only' committed to the 'restoration of the New Testament church in doctrine and life' by an appeal to 'the Bible alone as a rule of faith and practice' deserves the consideration of the whole Christian world in this new day."

North, James

"As long as people have an unreserved commitment to the authority of Scripture, we have a common platform on which to dialogue, even though we may infer different things from Scripture."

Nutt, Ziden

"Efforts may be made to negotiate peace between men on their own terms, legislate integration for ethnic groups, or write rules for ecumenicalism, but unity becomes a natural result when all bow before the authority of God and come under the blood of the cross where walls are broken down and all commune together as one in Christ."

"Biblical authority compels us to consider that it is time to rise above suspicions, bypass assumptions, and discover that we belong to one another in Christ in the unity of the Spirit."

"As I've traveled around the world, I know of many who used the Bible only and read themselves into agreeing with us about baptism and the Lord's Supper. I have yet to find anyone who independently read the Bible and became convicted that matters, which have divided the restoration movement, are doctrines necessitating division."

"Everyone is entitled to preferences, but God forbid that any would dishonor the authority of God's Word by dividing the church over personal preferences."

Olbricht, Tom

"The assembly is the place to show unity in Christ, for he came not only to bring at-one-ment with the Father but with the children of the Father."

Palmer, W. Robert

"Any congregation of believers existing today has the right to practice unity on the part of its members by declaring in word and practice that it wants to be that one church, no more and no less—the church of the New Testament."

Phillips, Marvin

> **"Let's unite on things specifically taught and be tolerant on things sincerely deducted."**

"Biblical unity is where God is honored and His Word respected—where the essentials are preached and opinions are tolerated."

"We should let the Judge be the judge and let the Father run the family."

"Let's unite on things specifically taught and be tolerant on things sincerely deducted."

Phillips, Thomas W.

"All systems have centers. The sun is the center of the solar system and God's Son is the center of the Christian system. . . . This central truth, that Jesus is the Christ, the Son of God, is the truth to be put before the world as the basis of union for all believers."

"The purest age of Christianity was that in which there was no creed but Christ."

Pile, William

"If unconditional love brought Jews and Gentiles together, it can bring the body of Christ together in our time with such force that the gates of hell will quiver."

"If denominational names don't really mean anything, then let's drop them. Answer everyone who asks, 'I'm just a Christian.'"

Reese, Jack R.

"Christians ought to be able to talk to one another."

"No one today is guilty for what happened a hundred years ago, but we are answerable for what we do now. . . . God has granted us the grace in our day to be instruments of peace."

Richardson, Robert

"The Christian faith . . . consists not in any theory or system of doctrine, but in a sincere belief in the person and mission of our Lord Jesus Christ."

Robinson, William

"The church began as a fellowship, and as one; and only as a united fellowship can she effectively do her work and bring peace into a distracted world."

Russell, Bob

"It is time for us to disregard the labels that isolate us and the creeds (written and unwritten) that separate us and fulfill Christ's prayer for unity. Denominational and other artificial divisions break the heart of God as surely as sibling disputes break the heart of a loving earthly father."

"It's time for all genuine believers to join forces and be one, so that the world might believe that Jesus is the Christ, the Son of the living God."

Scott, Walter

"The Bible contains one truth which is the sun to which all other Christian truths are planets in a spiritual solar system." ("Thou art the Christ, the Son of the Living God" Matt. 16:16). It is the creed of the Christian, the bond of Christian union, and the way of salvation."

Shelburne, Gene

"I dream of a unity in Christ's Body that includes every soul who fits Paul's description ("All those everywhere who call on the Lord Jesus Christ" 1 Cor. 1:2). Any concept of unity smaller than this is too small."

"When Jesus makes my enemy His friend, He makes that enemy my friend as well. Thus He reconciles us in His Body, not because of anything we have done, but by what He has done to save us both."

Statements

Shelly, Rubel

"We cannot predicate unity on issues. We must affirm it in Christ—in Christ alone."

"I just want to be a Christian! I want to acknowledge every other person in the world who is a Christian as my spiritual brother or sister."

Shepherd, J.W.

> "If we are in Christ, we cannot help being one with all who are in Christ."

"It requires no negotiation or arrangements among men to unite them as one in Christ. If we are in Christ, we cannot help being one with all who are in Christ."

Smith, F. LaGard

"If we wish to be granted elbow-room for out own understanding of God's will, then we must grant that same elbow-room to all of our brothers and sisters in Christ. In that way we honor and protect both our consciences and theirs. Let there be no doubt: *We will not answer eternally to anyone else for what we believe or for how we worship God; and no one will answer to us.*"

Sommer, Frederick

"The way to unite is to unite. We must first want unity, believe in it, make it a primary Christian value, as Jesus did. Of course, it must be Christian unity that we want."

"We must be most sensitive at the point of things held in common, instead of most sensitive at the point of differences."

"If unity is the right and desirable thing, give it the right of way."

"We must be persuaded that the way to unity is through fellowship, not through disfellowship—that the way to grow unity is to practice it in the things which we have in common. . . ."

"Many are still standing where we once stood, and may we not exercise the same forbearance with them as we once asked for ourselves?"

Staton, Knofel

"God has only one family with all members sharing the same seed (*sperma*, 1 John 3:9). By having the same Father, we are eternal siblings with each other whether we like it or not."

Stone, Barton W.

"Let every Christian begin the work of union in himself."

"The union of Christians is the will of God, the prayer of Jesus, and the means of bringing the world to believe in Jesus, therefore it must be right. That man is then engaged in a righteous work, who labors to promote this union. . . . But the man who acts a contrary part must be wrong, and engaged in a work in opposition to the will of God, the prayer of Jesus, and the salvation of the world."

"But should all the professors of Christianity reject their various creeds and names, and agree to receive the Bible alone, and be called by no other name than Christian, will this unite them? No: we are fully convinced that unless they all possess the spirit of that book and name, they are far, very far from Christian union."

"The scriptures will never keep together in union and fellowship and members not in the spirit of the scriptures, which spirit is love, peace, unity, forbearance, and cheerful obedience. This is the spirit of the great Head of the body. I blush for my fellows, who hold up the Bible as the bond of union yet make their opinions of it tests of fellowship; who plead for union of all Christians; yet refuse fellowship with such as dissent from their notions."

> "I blush for my fellows, who hold up the Bible as the bond of union yet make their opinions of it tests of fellowship."

"Let us move forward under the name Christian. Let all other names be discarded and forgotten."

Stone, Sam E.

"To be of one mind does not necessarily mean that we will agree on every opinion about the Bible. But surely it means we will agree that the Bible is God's Word, that it means what it says, and that we should obey it. Isn't that the one mind to which Scripture calls us?"

"When we care about God's family, as we do our own, it will be reflected in how we treat other members. Christian unity is everybody's job."

"Our question is, 'Why can't we *all* just be *Christians*? Why should we set ourselves apart from other believers? Why can't we all wear only Christ's name? We don't *want* to be another denomination. We don't *intend* to be one. Why should a person have to say, 'I'm this kind of Christian or that kind'? Why can't all of us lay aside *all* our labels? Why can't we just take God's Word as our sole authority, and simply wear the name of our Savior?"

Stram, Walter

"Division in the church world today is treason against Christ, and presents a tragic stumbling-block to the non-Christian."

Sweeney, William E.

"We are seeking to restore that which is both essential and universal in Christianity."

Thomas, Reggie

"Where the Bible speaks we must be willing to submit ourselves to God's Word in obedience. Where the Bible is silent and it's a matter of opinion, we must allow everybody the right to their own opinion. We must not make any church laws governing people when they have a right to their own opinion."

Walker, Dean E.

"Unity of Christians consists of that oneness in Christ in which Jesus and the Father are one."

"Christian unity, supported in a life of the love exhibited in Jesus, is the predicate upon which the mission of Christ will be fulfilled."

Warpula, Calvin

"All divisions end in the grave. There are no denominations or separate groups in heaven. Christians going to heaven together need to love each other and work together now. Until we reach the heavenly world, we should celebrate our agreements, minister together in all ways we conscientiously can, and continue to patiently, lovingly, and biblically work toward greater unity."

> "I can place no greater demands on you to be my brother than God puts on you to be His son."

"I can place no greater demands on you to be my brother than God puts on you to be His son."

"We should receive into communion all whom God will receive into heaven."

Waters, J. Ervin

"If an omniscient God accepts ignorant me at the foot of the cross in the blood of His Son, then I can accept ignorant you at the foot of the cross in the blood of His Son. If a holy God accepts weak and sinful me at the foot of the cross in the blood of His Son, then I can accept weak and sinful you at the foot of the cross in the blood of His Son."

"I say to you without shame and without fear that wherever my Father has a son or a daughter I have a brother and a sister, and I will acknowledge them as such."

Williamson, Dale A.

"Any effort at unity must be predicated on the individual qualities of lowliness, meekness, forbearance, and love. All effort without these important ingredients is doomed to failure."

Wilson, Seth

"Who can read Jesus' prayer for unity without feeling that an unbelieving world is the dreadful price we pay for our sinful divisions?"

"Christ is one and not divided. We cannot be perfectly united in and with Him without becoming united with each other. If we have the mind of Christ we will have the same mind, and so on through all the characteristics of the Christian which we receive from Christ Himself."

> "Unity must be in Christ. Any other kind of unity is not only hopeless, but worthless."

"Unity must be in Christ. Any other kind of unity is not only hopeless, but worthless."

"What unites a repentant sinner with Christ unites him with all other persons who are thus united with Christ."

"In faith (believing what the Lord has said) let us have unity; in opinion (deciding what the Lord has not decided for us) let us have liberty; in obedience to Him, loyalty and faithfulness; in all things, love."

"Let us determine that we will recognize no religious body but His body. Let us identify with no people but all of His people, even when that is not easy to do. Let us show that we belong to Christ, not to any party."

"We are brothers if we are children of the same Father, whether we like it or not. God wants us to like it and to act like it. And He wants me to say, 'If you belong to Christ, then I belong to you.' He wants me to feel this in my heart and to act in that manner."

If you belong to Christ,
And I belong to Christ,
Then we are together in Christ!

Chapter Nine

A NEW APPEAL FOR AN OLD IDEAL
A Plea for Unity
(Part I)

I remember the day as though it were yesterday: Christmas Day, 1952. I had gotten a new intermediate size Franklin football and had taken it outside to punt in the back yard of the library next to the church parsonage where we lived in the little town of Hamburg, Iowa. Suddenly I heard two cars squeal to a stop. I peeked through the bushes and saw two men, probably in their thirties, circling each other warily. They were cursing one another with words I had never heard before. One took a wild swing at the other and before I could say, "Jack Robinson!" they were both slugging each other with all the might they could muster. This was my first exposure to real violence, and I was scared to death. Even now I can still hear those sodden sounds of fist on flesh; can still see the crimson drops of blood splattered in the snow.

I hightailed it back to the church parsonage to get Dad. When we returned to the scene of battle the men were still at it, slugging and swearing to beat the band. I stood in the snow in wide-eyed wonder as my father, slight and slender, bareheaded in the winter wind, approached those two ruffians. He began to speak to them in a voice both gentle and firm, "Men, on this day—of all days in the year—you should not be fighting. This is a day of 'peace on earth, good will to men.' Couldn't you find a better way to solve your differences?"

As my father pleaded with those men to cease their fighting, I saw an amazing thing happen. Those two guys stopped fighting! They stood there gasping for breath, their heads hanging in shame. One finally offered to shake hands if the other would. He would and they did. Before I could say "Davy Crockett!" they were back in their cars and driving away.

I walked back home hand-in-hand with my Dad fully believing that what I had just seen was truly a miracle. Today I continue to thank God for that snowy, windswept Christmas day when I saw firsthand what Jesus meant when He said, "Blessed are the peacemakers for they shall be called the children of God." It birthed within me a holy desire to be a peacemaker because more than anything else I want to be called a child of God.

Several years ago, after reading "The Seven Promises of a Promise Keeper," I composed "The Seven Commitments of a Peacemaker." Peacemakers are committed to . . .

- Letting the peace of God rule in their hearts (Col. 3:15).
- Telling others the good news of peace with God through faith in Jesus Christ (Acts 10:36; Rom. 5:1).
- Recognizing as God's children all who are in Christ, regardless of race, sex, or culture (1 Cor. 12:13; Gal. 3:26-28).
- Accepting fellow believers who have conscientious differences of opinion (Rom. 14:1-4; 15:7).
- Ministering reconciliation between brethren who are at odds with each other (Gen. 13:8; Phil. 4:2).
- Making every effort to keep the unity of the Spirit in the bond of peace (Eph. 4:3).
- Living at peace with everyone and pursuing the things that make for peace (Rom. 12:18; 14:19).

God has always wanted His children to be at peace with each other and to be one in spirit and purpose. This unity is modeled in the relationship that exists between the members of the Godhead—God the Father, God the Son, and God the Holy Spirit. There is no discord or dissension between them. Even though they have different roles in the redemption of man, they are united in nature, spirit, and purpose.

> Friction and faction will never be found in the Godhead. There has never been and never will be disharmony among the Trinity.

Friction and faction will never be found in the Godhead. There has never been and never will be disharmony among the Trinity. The three major world religions, indeed, all religions, all churches, all believers, need to take a lesson from the marvelous unity of the Godhead.

Man himself is a marvel of unity, created with a body, soul, and spirit (1 Thess. 5:23). We were created to live together in unity. After

Adam was created, God said, "It is not good that man should be alone; I will make a helper comparable to him" (Gen. 2:19). And so woman was made and God said, "They shall become one flesh" (Gen. 2:24). Adam and Eve became one. Two hearts now beat as one. They were together, united, and God was pleased. Marriage is a beautiful model of unity. When asked about the matter of divorce, Jesus said, "Have you not read that He who made them at the beginning 'made them male and female,' and said, 'For this reason a man shall leave his father and mother and be joined to his wife, and the two shall become one flesh'? So then, they are no longer two but one flesh. Therefore what God has joined together, let not man separate" (Matt. 19:4-6). The reason God hates divorce is because it destroys the unity that He intended to exist between those He made one in flesh and spirit, and the godly offspring that He desired (Mal. 2:15,16). God wants His children who marry to live together forever in love and harmony. Every divorce that occurs is like plunging cold steel in the heart of God. It was no accident that Jesus chose the model of marriage to illustrate the unity that is to exist between Himself and His bride, the church (Eph. 5:22-32). The church that divides drives a dagger in the heart of Christ.

> Every divorce that occurs is like plunging cold steel in the heart of God. The church that divides drives a dagger in the heart of Christ.

God told Abraham that He would make him into a great nation and that through him and this new nation, all peoples of the earth would be blessed (Gen. 12:1-3). Abraham believed God and became the father of Isaac. Isaac became the father of Jacob, whose name was later changed to Israel. Jacob/Israel had twelve sons who became the leaders of the twelve tribes of the nation of Israel, the nation God had promised that He would make. Twelve tribes, yet they were one nation. Israel was never so great as when they rose up as one man, fought as one, and conquered as one. Moses reminded them that the reason they had become so great (even though they were one of the smallest nations on earth) was because of their covenant relationship with God (Deut. 4:7,8; 7:6-11). After one of Solomon's sons, Rehoboam, split the nation in two by failing to listen to the wise counsel of the elders, ten tribes formed the northern kingdom (Israel) and the two remaining tribes became the southern kindom (Judah). Sometimes they even went to war against one another, spilling the blood of their brethren. They had forgotten that through them all nations of the earth were to be blessed. Instead, they became a laughingstock to the nations. Eventually, Israel was deported to Assyria for 131 years of captivity (853–722 B.C), and Judah was deported to Babylonia for 155 years of captivity (715–560 B.C.). Yet, even in their miserable estate, God promised that some day they would become one nation again, serving together under one king (Ezek. 37:15-28). A remnant from Judah was allowed to return to Jerusalem in 536 B.C., because the Messiah was to come from Judah. God's desire for oneness would not be thwarted, even by the stubbornness and sinfulness of His children.

Enter Jesus! Though existing from all eternity, He burst onto the scene in the blaze of a star over Bethlehem, born of a virgin, born to give us second birth. He came, as predicted by the prophets of old, from the tribe of Judah, and the scepter belonged to Him. He would establish His kingdom, a kingdom that would never be destroyed or belong to another (Dan. 2:44). He said He would build His church, and not even the gates of hell would be able to prevail against it (Matt. 16:18). That means that members of His church, full of His compassion, would storm the gates of hell itself to snatch souls from the flames (Jude 23). Jesus was His name and redemption was His game—if we can call rescuing the perishing a game.

Now God's desire for unity would be fulfilled, once and for all, in the person and work of His only begotten Son. He had sent prophets, priests, and kings, but now Jesus became the true Prophet, Priest, and King. He fulfilled all the prophecies of the coming Messiah, sacrificed Himself for the sins of all mankind on the cross, and reigns as King of kings and Lord of lords over His church today.

It was not an easy task, but it was a task that He took on joyfully, enduring the cross, despising its shame, and sitting down at the right hand of the throne of God (Heb. 12:2). He came to seek and save the lost. All were lost in sin. All had sinned and fallen short of the glory of God. There was not a soul on earth then that did not need His cleansing blood, and there is not a soul on earth today that does not need to be cleansed from their sins through His blood shed on

Calvary (Rom. 3:23-25). The world of Jesus' day was divided into two primary groups: Jew and Gentile. Both were utterly, hopelessly lost in sin. Jesus came, not only to forgive their sin, making them right with God, but also to make them one with each other. He came to preach peace to them that were afar (Gentiles) and to them that were near (Jews). No words can better explain this than the words of the apostle Paul. "But now in Jesus Christ you who once were far off have been made near by the blood of Christ. For He Himself is our peace, who has made both one, and has broken down the middle wall of division between us, having abolished in His flesh the enmity, that is, the law of commandments contained in ordinances, so as to create in Himself one new man from the two, thus making peace, and that He might reconcile them both to God in one body through the cross, thereby putting to death the enmity" (Eph. 2:13-16).

The practical results of what happened at the cross took only a short time to actually be seen. At Pentecost, some sixty days after Christ died on the cross and arose from the grave, about three thousand people, mostly Jews or Jewish proselytes, gladly received the message of the crucified and resurrected Christ, repented of their sins, were baptized for the forgiveness of sins, received the gift of the Holy Spirit, and were added to the church in Jerusalem (Acts 2:37-47). Some time later, in the city of Caesarea, a devout man named Cornelius became the first Gentile convert to Christianity (Acts 10). Peter explained to the apostles and brethren in Jerusalem, "So if God gave them the same gift as he gave us, who believed in the Lord Jesus Christ, who was I to think that I could oppose God?" The Jerusalem church rejoiced in the news, saying, "So then, God has granted even the Gentiles repentance unto life" (Acts 11:17,18, NIV).

Now Jew and Gentile could be together in Christ. It got better. Everyone who professed his faith in Christ and was baptized into Christ became one in Christ: Jews, Greeks, slaves, freemen, males, females, barbarians, even Scythians (Gal. 3:26-28; Col. 3:11). The story of the Scythians is especially amazing. Occupying what is today southern Russian, these warriors were so violent that they would behead their enemies and use the skull as their canteens. But here we see them in the one body of Christ where "Christ is all, and is in all."

This is not to say that it was always smooth sailing for the fledgling church, made up of such diverse people. There were differences, disputes, and even some unfortunate divisions, especially in Corinth. Nevertheless, the early Christians were constantly urged by their leaders to love one another, bear with one another, be patient with one another, be kind to one another, pray for one another, serve one another, and accept one another. The only way they could do this was by possessing the mind of Christ and living by the power of the Holy Spirit. By one Spirit they had all been baptized into one body (1 Cor. 12:13). The fruit of the Spirit in their lives—something they could not produce on their own—was love, joy, peace, longsuffering, kindness, goodness, faithfulness, gentleness, and self-control (Gal. 5:22,23). As long as they lived in the Spirit, they were empowered to crucify the works of the flesh, those things that worked against unity—hatred, contentions, jealousies, outbursts of wrath, selfish ambition, dissension, heresies, etc.

Having the mind of Christ was also crucial to Christian unity. The first Christians were urged to be like-minded, to be of one accord, to be of one mind, in lowliness of mind to esteem others better than themselves. "Let this mind be in you which was also in Christ Jesus" (Phil. 2:5). Even though He was in very form God, Christ humbled Himself and became a servant. Pride is perhaps the greatest barrier to unity. When we have the mind of Christ, we will have the manners of Christ. Paul urged two early Christian women who couldn't seem to get along, Euodia and Syntche, to be of the same mind in the Lord (Phil. 2:2). Unity comes through humility, having the mind of Christ. When we think like Christ, we will act like Christ, for "as a man thinks, so is he." Most church disputes come from unchristian thinking, which leads to uncharitable behavior.

> Most church disputes come from unchristian thinking, which leads to uncharitable behavior.

God desires His children to be one. Christ made them one at the cross. The Holy Spirit gave us the gift of unity, for we are urged to "make every effort to keep the unity of the Spirit through the bond of peace" (Eph. 4:3). Unity is not ours to make or manufacture, it is simply ours to maintain. We are not to make "some" effort to keep this unity, we are to make "every" effort. We do that through the bond of peace. The Prince of Peace came and preached peace to those near and far. He made peace between all warring parties through the blood of His cross. He pronounces His blessing on those who are peace-makers—not those who are peace lovers or peace talkers, but those who make peace. Making peace is harder than making war, but it is well worth the effort. If my father could make two angry adults quit fighting on Christmas day, surely our Father in heaven is infinitely more capable of continuing to make peace with all men through the blood of His Son and by the power of His Spirit!

I refuse to believe that what God has desired since the creation of the world, what Jesus Christ accomplished at the cross, and what the Holy Spirit has given us to guard with all our might and main is impossible to have and enjoy today. It is my conviction that the unity for which Jesus prayed in John 17 began with the birth of His church in Acts 2, was broadened to include the Gentiles in Acts 10, and is intended for every man, woman, boy, and girl on planet earth to this very day. That unity, though severely tested at times, was clearly seen in the New Testament church and has continued through the centuries. God has not left Himself without witness. Not even for one day. Even in the darkest days of the church, when persecution raged from without and heresies devoured from within, the light of faith and the power of practice has always shown and been seen. This remarkable unity will continue unabated throughout eternity. John's vision should be our vision. "After this I looked and there before me was a great multitude that no one could count, from every nation, tribe, people and language, standing before the throne and in front of the Lamb. They were wearing white robes and were holding palm branches in their hands. And they cried out in a loud voice: 'Salvation belongs to our God, who sits on the throne, and to the Lamb'" (Rev. 7:9,10, NIV). The united church of Christ in heaven will be an innumerable, international, multilingual, jubilant church!

> If my father could make two men quit fighting, surely our Father in heaven is infinitely more capable.

I believe this is what drove Paul to his knees in praise when he wrote, "For this reason I kneel before the Father, from whom his whole family in heaven and on earth derives its name" (Eph. 3:14,15

NIV). The family of God is an interstellar family, including those already in heaven and those who remain faithful on earth.

My conviction is the same as Paul's—"There is one body" (Eph. 4:4). He did not say, wistfully, there *was* one body. Paul was not a defeatist, dwelling in the musty past, forever thinking of how it used to be. Nor did the apostle to the Gentiles say, wishfully, "There *should* be one body." Paul was not some visionary, dreaming of how it might be. At the prompting of the Holy Spirit, Paul boldly declared: "There is one body and one Spirit, just as you were called in one hope of your calling; one Lord, one faith, one baptism; one God and Father of all, who is above all, and through all, and in you all" (Eph. 4:4-6). Nowhere in the writings of Paul is there so powerful an expression of unity.

If there is more than one body, then there is more than one Spirit, more than one hope, more than one Lord, one faith, one baptism, and one God and Father of all. To deny any of the "magnificent seven" in Ephesians is to deny them all. More than one Spirit? Confusion! More than one hope? Consternation! More than one Lord? Controversy! More than one faith? Carnage! More than one baptism? Conflict! More than one God? Chaos!

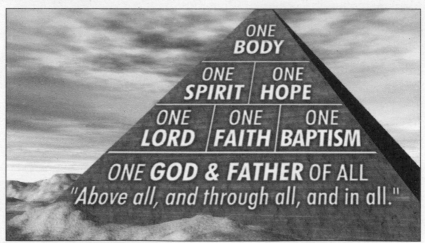

Think of a pyramid with me. Like a towering pyramid this passage rises from the heat of the desert floor. "The Great Pyramid of the Magnificent Seven." The Greek word for seven (*hepta*) corresponds to the Hebrew *sheba* which means "full" or "abundant." Seven was a sacred number to the Jews. Should we be surprised to find seven elements of unity in this Pauline passage? It is no accident or aberration. Paul did not use six expressions of unity for six is the number of man—incomplete, imperfect, lacking.

Looking at the accompanying four-tiered, seven-block pyramid, notice the "magnificent seven." The elongated base of our pyramid is where it all began—with God—"ONE God. "In the beginning GOD. . . ." And He is the FATHER of all, who is over all and through all and in all. The Father's family is an inclusive family.

The second tier reads, "One LORD, one FAITH, one BAPTISM." Jesus Christ is Lord of all. Faith in Him is the essence of that body of evidence known as "the faith that was once for all delivered to the saints" (Jude 3). We come into saving relationship with Him, and enjoy spiritual relationship with one another, through the one baptism (1 Cor. 12:13; Gal. 3:27).

The third tier speaks of "one SPIRIT" and "one HOPE." The Holy Spirit of God is that one Spirit, and the one hope appears to be the blessed hope that the first century Christians had—resurrection from the dead at the return of Jesus when He comes to take us home to heaven.

Now look at the capstone—"one BODY." It looms above like the gleaming tip of an iceberg on the ocean, like an unfurled flag flying from a mountain castle. I have always been impressed that Paul started with "one body" rather than with "one God." Perhaps it was because God is invisible but the church is visible. People judge God by the church! Our unity in Christ (or lack thereof) sends a | Our unity in Christ (or lack thereof) sends a powerful signal to the world. |
powerful signal to the world. We are visible. But are we credible?

The world at its worst needs the church at her best!

But I would be remiss if I did not point out, as Paul surely did, that the seven cardinal doctrines for the unity of the church are preceded by five vital attitudes. These attitudes serve as pillars or posts to support Paul's platform of doctrinal unity. Remove them and the whole platform collapses. Positional truth (belief) must be shored up by practical truth (behavior). Even when we are right on doctrine we can be wrong in attitude. More churches divide over bad attitudes than

> "I've never had to apologize for our position, but I've often had to apologize for our disposition."

faulty doctrine. So Paul writes, "Be completely humble and gentle; be patient, bearing with one another in love" (Eph. 4:2, NIV). Wayne Smith said, "I've never had to apologize for our position, but I've often had to apologize for our disposition." Pride has and can destroy all our preachments, no matter how correct they may be. So it begins with HUMILITY—*complete* humility—as it was with Christ when He humbled Himself and became a servant, washing His disciples' feet, touching the flesh of lepers, allowing His flesh to be nailed to the cross. The Latin word for humility is *humus*—the earth beneath our feet. No wonder the meek shall inherit the earth! They've been trodden down until they are almost a part of it. Peter instructs all to clothe themselves with humility (1 Pet. 5:5). Humility is something we put on. It is a spiritual garment. But what kind of garment? For some it is a greatcoat, for others a string bikini. Humility has not been our strong suit.

We are to be GENTLE with each other. When George Herbert Walker Bush was elected as the forty-first president of the United States in 1988, he said he wanted a "kinder and gentler America." Even though Paul, Silas, and Timothy had serious situations to deal with in the church of the Thessalonians, they stated, "But we were gentle among you, like a mother caring for her little children" (1 Thess. 2:7, NIV). I remember to this day my mother's spirit, words, and touch. Gentleness is a fruit of the Spirit. Paul made his appeal to the church of God in Corinth "by the meekness and gentleness of Christ" (1 Cor. 10:1). Think of how gentle Jesus was with the woman caught in adultery and the woman who crashed the party to wash His feet with her tears. Paul told young Timothy that he must be kind to everyone; even those who opposed him were to be instructed with gentleness (2 Tim. 2:24,25). I must confess that in my early years of ministry I was not all that gentle in my teaching.

The third vital predoctrinal attitude we must have is PATIENCE. Again, this too is a fruit of the Spirit. Do you see why it is so important to have the gift of the Holy Spirit living within us—why we must daily be led by the Spirit and walk in the Spirit? Left to ourselves we will become impatient with others, turning many away from Christ forever. God is a God of patience and we must emulate Him at every occasion. Think of how patient Christ was with His disciples. The two men who accompanied Christ on the road to Emmaus were "slow of heart to believe" yet Christ agreed to stay with them for supper until their eyes were opened (Luke 24:25-32). Think of how long it took you to see the truth. Can we not be more patient with people when they are slow to believe?

We are also to bear with one another. Some translations use the word FORBEARANCE, which means to endure, to bear up under, to refrain from doing something, to hold back. It means putting up with people we'd like to put down. God is called a God of forbearance (Rom. 2:4; 3:25). Christ put up with much grief, not only from His bickering disciples but also from His bitter enemies. Forbearance is kin to longsuffering, another fruit of the Spirit. Forbearance is the forerunner to forgiveness: "bearing with one another, if anyone has a complaint against another; even as Christ forgave you, so you also must do" (Col. 3:13). In a sermon that was prepared but never delivered because of his sudden death, Donald G. Hunt wrote, "It's impossible to forgive until you learn to forbear."

> "It's impossible to forgive until you learn to forbear."

The final spiritual attitude that precedes the doctrinal platform for unity is LOVE, mentioned more than three hundred times in Scripture. Though mentioned last in Ephesians 4:3, it is mentioned first in several passages exalting this much-needed virtue. For example:

♦ "But the fruit of the Spirit is love, joy, peace, longsuffering, kindness, goodness, faithfulness, gentleness, self-control" (Gal. 5:22,23).
♦ "But above all these things put on love, which is the bond of perfection" (Col. 3:14).
♦ "And above all things have fervent love for one another, for 'love will cover a multitude of sins'" (1 Pet. 4:8).

Love is cited first because there is no greater thing than love. "And now abides faith, hope, love, these three; but the greatest of these is love" (1 Cor. 13:13). Homer H. Halley called love the premier teaching of Christianity, the church's most effective weapon, the

133

essence of God's character, the most powerful force in the universe. Love is all of that and more.

A church may profess all the marks of being a New Testament church, but if love is missing then they have missed the mark. Jesus said, "A new commandment I give to you, that you love one another; as I have loved you, that you also love one another. By this all will know that you are My disciples, if you have love for one another" (John 13:34,35). Here we see that love is a *mandate* from Christ: "love one another" is a commandment! Love is an action, not a feeling. Some are "missing in action" in this regard. Christ is the divine *model* of love: "as I have loved you." Christ loved His disciples to the bitter end (John 13:1). Love is also the *mark* of a true Christian: "all will know that you are My disciples." Love is the Christian's "coat of arms" by which others will recognize him or her as a fellow Christian.

> A church may profess all the marks of being a New Testament church, but if love is missing then they have missed the mark.

Don DeWelt, the founder of *One Body*, a magazine I have edited since its inception in 1984, wrote a wonderful piece he called "His Love," a paraphrase of 1 Corinthians 13.

His Love

If I speak or write with the tongues of scholarship and orthodoxy and yet His body is torn with division, I am only disturbing the airwaves and wasting ink.

If I have the gift of prophecy and can fathom all mysteries and all knowledge and yet do nothing about the hatred, ignorance and misunderstanding among His children, I am exactly nothing.

If I have the greatest of confidence in my position and our plea for the truth and yet ignore the terrible factions and divisions in His body, there is no gain for me—only a terrible loss!

HIS LOVE is patient, very patient with those who disagree.

HIS LOVE is kind while listening to or talking with those who contradict us.

HIS LOVE is perfectly willing that everyone else get the credit if only we can be united in one divine body.

HIS LOVE boasts in the Lord, not in our size or influence.

HIS LOVE is exceeding proud of the beauty of the one vine and the one flock and the one vinedresser and the one shepherd.

HIS LOVE is so very careful to save the dignity of every man and his opinion—otherwise there can be no communication.

HIS LOVE lays down gladly all desire to seek his own way that each of us might have opportunity to seek together His way.

HIS LOVE refuses to be angry—even where much time has elapsed and no one seems to care or understand. Our Lord treats us this way.

HIS LOVE has a tremendous capacity for forgetfulness. No record of wrong is kept—it is enough to know You so we can talk with clear conscience to each other.

HIS LOVE takes no satisfaction in those who have less in their fellowship than we do—but rather is broken down before You over the sad fact that we are not even keeping with the birth rate in the conversion of the lost world.

HIS LOVE is ecstatic over every report of progress in efforts at unity.

HIS LOVE always protects those who have any interest at all in reaching out to others with a desire to understand.

HIS LOVE always wants to trust those who express their love in the name of our Lord even when sad experience tells them love is not always sincere.

HIS LOVE springs eternal in the hearts of those who love the oneness of His body. Such love exceeds their own personal interests.

HIS LOVE keeps right on loving—on and on in the face of impossible, irritable odds—for this is how You love us, and so we should love each other.

HIS LOVE will never fail! Let us love one another even as He loved us! When we do we shall be one and the world shall be won!

Our position must be biblical truth and our spiritual disposition must be His! The "acid test" of our Christianity is whether or not we live out the truth of love's particulars, as spelled out for us in 1 Corinthians 13:4-7. Every time the word "love" appears, replace it with your name. For example: "Victor is patient, Victor is kind. Victor does not envy, Victor does not boast, Victor is not proud. Victor is not rude, Victor is not self-seeking, Victor is not easily angered, Victor keeps no record of wrongs. Victor does not delight in evil, but Victor rejoices with the truth. Victor always protects, Victor always trusts, Victor always hopes, Victor always perseveres."

Together in Christ we must:

Love one another as Christ loves us,
Speak the truth in love as He did,
Practice love every day and in every way.

Chapter Ten

A NEW APPEAL FOR AN OLD IDEAL
A PLEA FOR UNITY
(PART II)

My father had a great "radio voice." Sometimes on Friday nights he would turn the lights down low and read stories to us five children. I especially liked it when he would read the thrilling tales of Sherlock Holmes, creating separate voices for the detective's intrepid companion, Dr. Watson, and even the evil Professor Moriarty. We also had family devotions every weeknight with all of us reading from the Bible, then kneeling and praying together as a family.

One night when I was about fifteen, I got up to get a drink of water. The bedroom door of my parents was partially open and I could see them kneeling by their bed. They were praying for me! Although I had become a Christian at age twelve, I was not all that I should be as a Christian young man. I can still see that sacred scene and can still hear the urgency in their voices as they prayed for me to make full surrender to Christ.

Robert McCheyne (1813–1843) said, "If I could hear Christ praying for me in the next room, I would not fear a million enemies. Yet distance makes no difference. He is praying for me!" Christ is still in the "next room" praying for us for "He ever lives to make intercession" (Heb. 7:15). But there was also a night—O what a night it was—when Jesus prayed for you and me. It was the greatest prayer ever prayed.

That poignant prayer still rings in our ears today, some two thousand years later. "I do not pray for these alone, but also for those who will believe in Me through their word; that they all may be one, as You, Father, are in Me, and I in You; that they also may be one in Us, that the world may believe that You sent Me" (John 17:20,21).

The person who is not touched and moved by His prayer has yet to know the heart of Christ.

The person who is not touched and moved by His prayer has yet to know the heart of Christ.

This priceless prayer focuses on four objects: Christ Himself, the Word of God, the unity of all believers, and the evangelization of the world.

All who are together in Christ, or desire to be together in Christ, can and should agree on these four elements of His dying prayer: *the centrality of Christ, the authority of Scripture, the necessity of unity, the urgency of evangelism.*

The Centrality of Christ

Our Lord prayed for those who would believe on Him. "I pray . . . for those who will believe *in Me*" (John 17:20b). There is much we can and should believe, but there is one thing we *must* believe. The greatest question of all time was asked by Jesus Himself, "What do you think about the Christ? Whose Son is He?" (Matt. 22:42). The answer to that question was given by the apostle Peter, in what we sometimes call the Good Confession, "You are the Christ, the Son of the living God" (Matt. 16:16).

Should any other confession be asked of us than what Jesus required of them? We believe that the Petrine confession, "You are the Christ, the Son of the living God," is sufficient.

To confess that Jesus is the Christ is to state that we believe He is God's promised Messiah of the Old Testament, the One chosen of God to be the Savior of the world.

To confess that He is the Son of the living God is to state that we believe He is God's only begotten Son, and that whoever believes in Him shall not perish, but have everlasting life.

There should be no other creed but Christ. The word "creed" is Latin for "I believe." No Christian in the New Testament era was ever asked to make any other confession than "I believe that Jesus is the Christ, the Son of the living God." This is why we have stated that there should be "no creed but Christ."

> No Christian in the New Testament era was ever asked to make any other confession than "I believe that Jesus is the Christ."

Whoever He said He was, this we believe. Whatever He said He would do, this we believe. Whatever He said He will do in the future, this we believe.

The person who confesses his or her faith in Jesus Christ, and is baptized into Christ, becomes a Christian and should gladly be known from that day forward as a Christian.

- "And the disciples were first called *Christians* in Antioch" (Acts 11:26).
- "You almost persuade me to become a *Christian*" (Acts 26:28).
- "Yet if anyone suffers as a *Christian*, let him not be ashamed, but let him glorify God in this matter" (1 Pet. 4:16).

But being known as a "Christian" means that we must live up to that "noble name" by which we are called. Far too many, by their shameful speech and careless conduct, have brought reproach upon the One whose name they wear.

To be a Christian means that we will manifest His character and conduct in our every waking hour. We will let His mind be in us. We will allow His word to richly dwell in us. We will speak as He would have us speak, do as He would have us do, go where He would have us go. The things that stirred Him will stir us. The things that did not stir Him will not stir us. What was an issue to Jesus will be our issue. What was not an issue to Jesus will not become an issue with us.

> What was an issue to Jesus will be our issue. What was not an issue to Jesus will not become an issue with us.

The cross of Christ will be central in the preaching of the church. Yes, it will remain "foolishness to those who are perishing, but to us who are being saved it is the power of God" (1 Cor. 1:18). We will "preach Christ crucified," even though it will be a stumbling block to some and foolishness to others. We will, with the apostles of old, determine "not to know anything among you except Jesus Christ and Him crucified" (1 Cor. 2:2). Any "glorying" in the church will be "in the cross of our Lord Jesus Christ, by whom the world has been crucified to me, and I to the world" (Gal. 6:14). This means we will do more than *preach* the message of the cross—we will *live* the message of the cross, even though it proves to be painful to the flesh.

Everything we do as a Christian, individually, and as a congregation, corporately, will be centered in Jesus Christ, for "Christ is all, and is in all." If it is not connected to Christ, what business does it have in the life of a Christian or in the life of a Christian church? For example:

- A living, growing relationship with Christ is vital, for we are to abide in Him (John 15:4).
- The words of Christ are to abide in us (John 15:7) and richly dwell in us (Col. 3:16).
- Coming to the Father through Jesus' name is essential to an effective prayer life (John 15:16).
- We are to remember Christ always, but especially at the time of communion, or Lord's Supper (1 Cor. 11:24,25).
- The commands of Christ are to be given highest priority, such as the Great Commission, discipleship, baptism, and postbaptismal instruction (Matt. 28:19,20).

Our Lord said He would build His church (Matt. 16:18), and we believe that church came into existence on the Day of Pentecost, A.D. 30 (Acts 2:1-47). God made Christ to be the head over His church, which is His body (Eph. 1:22,23), and there is only one body (Eph 4:4). One body is all that was ever intended, all that ever was built, all that now exists, for Christ is not divided (1 Cor. 1:13). All who are

> If a person is "in Christ," he cannot be any other place than "in Christ."

in Christ are in His body and have fellowship with Him. They also have fellowship with others in that same local body of believers and they are one in spirit with all other baptized believers throughout the world, even if they never meet them this side of heaven. If a person is "in Christ," he cannot be any other place than "in Christ."

Each Christian congregation has the right to govern itself by following the teachings of Christ to the best of their understanding and ability. In the New Testament the autonomy of one church was never usurped by another church. Each congregation elected their own leaders and conducted the Christ-centered worship, teaching, and mission of the church without being told how to by outsiders. Today every church on the face of the earth has the right to govern their own affairs, following the teachings and spirit of their head, Jesus Christ. Every church on every continent can be the one body of Christ if they choose to be. In both structure and spirit they can be Christians only, all the while remembering that they

> Every church on every continent can be the one body of Christ if the members choose to be.

are not the only Christians. Only God Himself knows the hearts of those who are truly His.

Today some churches are dropping their distinctive denominational names. We believe that is a step in the right direction, but only if those who do so are doing so from pure motives, desiring to be simply Christians. How much easier it would be for weary seekers of spiritual truth in the world if every church they sought out was wearing the name of Christ alone, teaching the message of Christ alone, doing the work of Christ alone!

Together, yes, but together "in Christ!" Let's be glad to wear His name, lift up His cross, teach His word, manifest His spirit, remember His sacrifice, and carry out His commission!

The Authority of Scripture

Our Lord prayed that people might come to faith in Him "through their word" (John 17:20c). He had already prayed that His disciples would be sanctified (set apart) by the truth of God's word (John 17:17). Now He prays that those select disciples would teach and preach in such a manner that all people would come to believe that He indeed was who they proclaimed Him to be, the Christ, the Son of the living God. Our initial faith in Christ does not come from out of the blue. "So then faith comes by hearing, and hearing by the word of God" (Rom. 10:17). What the apostles preached about Christ eventually became known as the "apostles' doctrine" (Acts 2:42). The apostles were quick to point out, however, that the message they proclaimed was not merely a message from men. "For this reason we also thank God without ceasing, because when you received the word of God which you heard from us, you welcomed it not as the word of men, but as it is in truth, the word of God, which also effectively works in you who believe" (1 Thess. 2:13).

The word of God as preached by the apostles was the reason the early church grew with such rapidity. Those who gladly received the word on Pentecost (about three thousand souls) were baptized (Acts 2:41). That number quickly grew to five thousand when "many of those who heard the word believed" (Acts 4:4). From that point on the record simply says, "And the word of God spread, and the number of the disciples multiplied greatly in Jerusalem" (Acts 6:7).

The apostles were all preaching the same message, Jesus Christ.

- "God has made this Jesus, whom you crucified, both Lord and Christ" (Acts 2:36).
- ". . . they taught the people and preached in Jesus the resurrection from the dead" (Acts 4:2).
- "Nor is there salvation in any other, for there is no other name under heaven given among men by which we must be saved" (Acts 4:12).
- "And daily in the temple, and in every house, they did not cease teaching and preaching Jesus as the Christ" (Acts 5:42).

The word that the apostles proclaimed was "that Christ died for our sins according to the Scriptures, and that He was buried, and that he rose again the third day according to the Scriptures" (1 Cor. 15:3,4). *According to the Scriptures!* That is key to understanding the growth and unity of the New Testament church, then and now! The Scriptures are our sole authority for knowing about Christ, coming to faith in Christ, being baptized into union with Christ, and sharing our faith in Christ with others.

The theme of all Scripture is Christ. Jesus declared, "You search the Scriptures, for in them you think you have eternal life; and these are they which testify of Me" (John 5:39). The theme of the Bible is Jesus. In the Old Testament, "Someone is coming." In the Gospels, "Someone has come." In the Epistles, and in particular, Revelation, "Someone is coming again." From beginning to end the Holy Scriptures point us to Christ.

The Scriptures are our sole authority for becoming a Christian. No single passage contains all that one must do to become a Christian but the terms of pardon can never be fewer than what are expressed in any passage. On the *divine* side there is God's grace (Eph. 2:8) and mercy

(Titus 3:5). There is also Jesus Himself (Matt. 1:21) and His blood (Rev. 1:5). Then there is the saving gospel (1 Cor. 15:1,2) and the preaching of the cross (1 Cor. 1:21). On the *human* side, man's response to the gospel of grace, there is the matter of faith in Christ (John 3:16), repentance toward Christ (Acts 20:21) confession of Christ (Acts 8:37), baptism into Christ (Gal. 3:22), and living for Christ (Gal. 2:20).

The Scriptures are our sole authority for living the Christian life. Most of the New Testament contains postbaptismal teachings on how to live. The key to a successful Christian life is the indwelling gift of the Holy Spirit, imparted to us at our baptism (Acts 2:38). The eighth chapter of Romans may be one of the most important chapters in all of Scripture for Christian living. Those who are now "in Christ" live "according to the Spirit" (v. 1). Three times we are told that the Spirit of God dwells in us; in fact, "if anyone does not have the Spirit of Christ, he is not His" (v. 9). Through the power of the Spirit, we are enabled to put to death the deeds of the body (v. 13). The indwelling Spirit reminds us that we are God's children (v. 14,16). He helps us in all our weaknesses, even interceding for us when we don't know how to pray as we should (v. 26,27).

The Holy Spirit is the one whom Jesus promised would come to help us in our every need (John 14:26; 15:26; 16:13). He is the one who transforms us into the image of Christ (2 Cor. 3:18), strengthens us in our inner life (Eph. 3:16), and sheds abroad God's love in our hearts (Rom. 5:5). The Christian who sincerely walks in the Spirit will not fulfill the lust of the flesh or engage in the works of the flesh: sexual immorality, impurity, debauchery, idolatry, witchcraft, hatred, discord, jealousy, fits of rage, selfish ambition, dissension, factions, envy, drunkenness, orgies, and the like (Gal. 5:19-21). Such ungodly behavior will bar us from the eternal kingdom of God. "Do you not know that the unrighteous will not inherit the kingdom of God? Do not be deceived. Neither fornicators, nor idolaters, nor adulterers, nor homosexuals, nor sodomites, nor thieves, nor covetous, nor drunkards, nor revilers, nor extortioners will inherit the kingdom of God" (1 Cor. 6:9,10). Paul did not say, "That's what some of you *are*. It's O.K. We're not here to judge." Rather he declared, "And such *were* some of you. But you were washed, but you were sanctified, but you were justified in the name of our Lord Jesus and by the Spirit of our God"

(1 Cor. 6:11). The Spirit of God does not justify sinful behavior or relationships, whether homosexual or heterosexual. Same-sex "marriage," which is being blessed and sanctified by some mainline denominations today, destroys the beautiful picture of Christ and the church (Eph. 5:31-33). It presents a distorted and corrupt imitation of marriage. As long as we are led by the Spirit and live in the Spirit, we will never practice the works of the flesh, grieve the Holy Spirit (Eph. 4:32), or quench the Holy Spirit's power in our lives (1 Thess. 5:17).

The Scriptures are the sole authority for charting the course of the church. Those called to be Christians are called to be the church (*ekklesia*), "called out." God has called us out of a world of sin to be His new society, the church. *Ekklesia* is used 114 times in the New Testament, referring either to the universal church (Eph. 1:22,23) or to a local congregation of believers (1 Cor. 1:2). The founder of the church is Christ (Matt. 16:18). The foundation of the church is Christ (1 Cor. 3:11). The head of the church is Christ (Col. 1:18), and He has all authority in the church (Matt. 28:18). Those belonging to the church were called Christians (Acts 11:26). Everywhere they went they preached Christ (Acts 5:42). The message of the church was Christ and Him crucified (1 Cor. 2:2). The ordinances of the church are Christian baptism (Matt. 28:19) and the Lord's Supper (Luke 22:19,20). The primary mission of the church is to preach the gospel of Christ to every creature (Mark 16:15). The identifying mark of the church is love for fellow Christians (John 13:34,35). The destiny of the church is to live with Christ forever (John 14:3).

There may be more that the church can and should do, but these Bible-based, Christ-centered beliefs and practices can serve as starters. Every church on earth is free to be the body of Christ, simply Christians and Christians only, doing His will and work to the best of their understanding and ability. The more congregations return to the model of the New Testament church, the more they will resemble New Testament Christianity in the twenty-first century. A mutual commitment to Scripture and Scripture alone will help us answer our Lord's dying prayer.

> The more congregations return to the model of the New Testament church, the more they will resemble New Testament Christianity in the twenty-first century.

How firm a foundation, ye saints of the Lord,
Is laid for your faith in His excellent Word!
What more can He say than to you He hath said,
To you who for refuge to Jesus have fled?
        Rippon's *Selection of Hymns*, 1787

THE NECESSITY OF UNITY

Our Lord prayed that all who would believe in Him through the word would be one. "That they all may be one . . ." (John 17:21a). The subjects of His prayer have now changed from the twelve that He chose to be His disciples to an innumerable multitude of believers in the future. He began by praying for His immediate disciples, but now He prays for all that will believe in Him. This is the night Jesus prayed for His church that was yet to be built. He knew that His church must be a *united* church or all was lost.

Jesus prayed for *all* believers—"for those who will believe in Me . . . that they *all* may be one." No church or denomination can claim this prayer for themselves alone. Such a claim would be selfish and ludicrous. The same God that wants all people to repent and believe wants all believers to be one.

> No church or denomination can claim this prayer for themselves alone.

The prayer of Jesus is both inclusive and exclusive. It is inclusive in that He prayed for all to be one. It is exclusive in that He prayed for those who believe in Him through the word. Not everyone accepts the authority of Scripture. Not everyone believes that Jesus is the Christ, the Son of the living God. Some preach the Bible without preaching Christ. Some believe that Jesus was a historical figure, a good man who did good things and spoke wonderful words, but do not believe that He is the divine Savior of the world, i.e., the Christ of Scripture.

Our unity in Christ shows that we are all God's children. "For you are all sons of God through faith in Christ Jesus. For as many of you as were baptized into Christ have put on Christ. There is neither Jew nor Greek, there is neither slave nor free, there is neither male nor female; for you are all one in Christ Jesus" (Gal. 3:26-28).

Our unity in Christ is a gift of the Spirit. "For by one Spirit we were all baptized into one body—whether Jews or Greeks, whether slaves or free—and have all been made to drink into one Spirit" (1 Cor. 12:13). This precious gift is to be maintained at all cost. Every Christian is urged, "Make every effort to keep the unity of the Spirit in the bond of peace" (Eph. 4:3, NIV).

Our unity in Christ calls us to live in peace with one another, in spite of our diverse backgrounds. ". . . there is neither Greek nor Jew,

> Our unity in Christ calls us to live in peace with one another, in spite of our diverse backgrounds.

circumcised nor uncircumcised, barbarian, Scythian, slave nor free, but Christ is all and in all. Therefore, as the elect of God, holy and beloved, put on tender mercies, kindness, humbleness of mind, meekness, longsuffering; bearing with one another, and forgiving one another, if anyone has a complaint against another; even as Christ forgave you, so you also must do. But above all these things put on love, which is the bond of perfection. And let the peace of God rule in your hearts, to which also you were called in one body; and be thankful" (Col. 3:11-15).

Our unity in Christ is commanded of us. The New Commandment states, "Love one another, as I have loved you" (John 13:34). We are not at liberty to love when we feel like it or love only those who love us in return. The One who has "all authority" has issued the command. Scripture commands that we be one in Christ, and that we shun anything that smacks of division. For example:

- "Therefore receive one another, just as Christ received us, to the glory of God" (Rom. 15:7).
- "Now I plead with you, brethren, by the name of our Lord Jesus Christ, that you all speak the same thing, and that there be no divisions among you, but that you be perfectly joined together in the same mind and in the same judgment" (1 Cor. 1:10).
- ". . . there should be no schism in the body, but that the members should have the same care for one another" (1 Cor. 12:25).
- "Be kind and compassionate to one another, forgiving each other, just as in Christ God forgave you" (Eph. 4:32, NIV).
- "If you have any encouragement from being united with Christ . . . then make my joy complete by being like-minded, having the same love, being one in spirit and purpose. Do

146

nothing out of selfish ambition or vain conceit, but in humility consider others better than yourselves" (Phil. 2:1-3, NIV).

Our unity in Christ should follow the winsome example of the Father and the Son. "That they all may be one, *as You, Father, are in Me, and I in You; that they also may be one in us* . . ." (John 17:21b). Jesus and the Father are one (John 10:30). We have the divine promise that if we love Christ and keep His word, both the Father and the Son will come to us and make their home with us (John 14:23). In a Christian home, there is unity. Should it be any different in a Christian church? The more we realize that we are in a spiritual relationship with Christ and God, the more winsome our spirit and behavior will be. Although we are not divine in nature, as are the Father and the Son, we can be "partakers of the divine nature" (2 Pet. 1:4). The more we partake of the divine nature, the more spiritual we will become. The more we focus on externals, opinions, and other people, the less spiritual we will be. Those who hunger and thirst for righteousness will be filled (Matt. 5:6). Those who hunger for lesser things will always be empty. And since nature abhors a vacuum, those who are empty are in peril of being filled with something not of God (Luke 11:26). When we are filled with the fullness of God, there can be no more room for anything else. So the way to a more perfect unity with one another is for all of us, individually and corporately, to ask God to answer Paul's prayer for the Christians in Ephesus in our own lives and churches. "For this reason I bow my knees to the Father of our Lord Jesus Christ, from whom the whole family in heaven and earth is named, that He would grant you, according to the riches of His glory . . .

- to be strengthened with might through His Spirit in the inner man,
- that Christ may dwell in your hearts through faith;
- that you, being rooted and grounded in love, may be able to comprehend with all the saints what is the width and length and depth and height—to know the love of Christ which passes knowledge;
- that you may be filled with all the fullness of God" (Eph. 3:14-19).

Rise up, O Church of God!
Have done with lesser things;
Give heart and mind and soul and strength
To serve the King of kings.
                              William P. Merrill

The Urgency of Evangelism

Finally, our Lord prayed, "that the world may believe that You sent Me" (John 17:21c). This awesome truth is repeated a few verses later. "I in them, and You in Me; that they may be made perfect in one, and that the world may know that You have sent Me, and have loved them as You have loved Me" (John 17:23). *That the world may believe! That the world may know!* Here we find yet another focus for Jesus' prayer. It is not for Himself. It is not for His disciples. It is not for us. It is for the world! This does not contradict His earlier statement, "I do not pray for the world" (John 17:9). In that context He was praying for His disciples to be sanctified so they would be prepared to be sent into the world. But at this point in His prayer, Christ has the world on His heart. This is especially seen in John's gospel.

- "For God so loved the *world* that He gave His only begotten Son . . ." (3:16).
- "For God did not send His Son into the *world* to condemn the *world,* but that the *world* through Him might be saved" (3:17).
- "Now we believe, not because of what you have said, for we have heard for ourselves and know that this is indeed the Christ, the Savior of the *world*" (4:42).
- "I am the living bread which came down from heaven . . . and the bread is My flesh, which I shall give for the life of the *world*" (6:51).
- "I am the light of the *world*. He who follows Me shall not walk in darkness, but have the light of life" (8:12).

No wonder Mark's account of the Great Commission reads, "Go into all the *world* and preach the gospel to *every* creature" (Mark 16:16). Jesus Christ is a world Savior and He wants the whole world to be saved. He came into the world to seek and save the lost (Luke 19:10). He came into the world to save sinners, even those who consider themselves the worst of sinners (1 Tim. 1:15). He is the Lamb slain from the foundation of the world (Rev. 13:8).

The reason Jesus prayed for the unity of all believers was for the purpose of the world. "That they all may be one . . . that the world may believe . . . that the world may know. . . ." Our disunity has been a disservice to the world. They deserve better. They deserve the best. God gave them His best. Are we giving them our best? Will we give them our best? Many a lost soul has pointed a finger of accusation at a divided church. "If you people who claim to be Christians can't get

> Our disunity has been a disservice to the world. They deserve better.

along, why should I come and join you? I've got enough troubles of my own." Mahatma Gandhi is said to have rejected Christianity because of the bad behavior of some Christians.

There is a greater purpose than unity in Christ in this prayer. The reason Jesus prayed for our oneness is so that the world would see the heavenly unity modeled in the church and would recognize us as His true disciples, bearing His message that is true. "By this will all know that you are My disciples, if you have love for one another" (John 13:35). We are the visible body of Christ, but are we the credible body of Christ?

For the sake of a lost world Jesus came to save, we must come to our senses and do our best to come to a consensus on the essentials of the faith.

On November 22, 1963, President John F. Kennedy was assassinated in Dallas, Texas. Within a few hours the whole world knew that the young president had been slain. Yet (God forgive us), two millennia have come and gone and half the people in the world still do not know that Christ died for their sins. Isn't it time we get serious about this matter?

Jesus prayed another prayer that is equally important. It came from His heart of compassion for people. "And Jesus went about all the cities and villages, teaching in their synagogues, preaching the gospel of the kingdom, and healing every sickness and every disease among the people. But when He saw the multitudes, He was moved with compassion for them, because they were weary and scattered, like sheep having no shepherd. Then He said to His disciples,

- "The harvest truly is plentiful, but the laborers are few."
- "Therefore pray the Lord of the harvest to send out laborers into His harvest" (Matt. 9:37,38).

Let us lift up our eyes from lesser things. Let us look at the harvest fields—*His* harvest fields! Look, "for they are already white for harvest!" Listen, for someone is praying that the Lord of the harvest would send laborers into His harvest! Perhaps it is some poor lost soul praying that someone would come to them with a

> Let us look at the harvest fields — His harvest fields — "already white for harvest!"

message of hope. Before dawn on November 4, 1956, Russian tanks rolled into Budapest. A Hungarian radio broadcaster made a dramatic appeal: "We don't have much time. You know what is happening. Help the Hungarian nation, help its workers, its peasants, and its intellectuals. Help! Help! Help!" The radio went silent and soon ten thousand Hungarians lay dead in the streets.

Perhaps it is some weary worker who has labored long and hard and needs someone to come and help him reap the harvest.

Perhaps it is the Lord Himself praying that His people would at last go together into His harvest fields to reap that which has been rotting for far too long.

Many years ago Walter E. Stram told this story. A child was lost in the great Dakota grain fields and scattering searchers failed to find the child. Finally, they joined hands and combed the fields systematically. In the cold hours of the next morning they found the child—dead. The mother cried, "Oh, why didn't we think to join hands sooner?"

Together in Christ, let us join hands and enter His harvest fields.

- To honor His prayer.
- For the sake of our children and grandchildren.
- For the sake of those who are lost in darkness and sin.
- Because we are all going to the grave.
- Because He is coming again.
- Because we must appear at the Judgment Seat of Christ.
- Because eternity is too long not to do otherwise!

I love the story of Joseph. He is a type of Jesus Christ—loved by his father, rejected by his brethren, sold for silver, condemned unjustly, numbered with transgressors, given up for dead, raised to rule, and became a Savior. But before Joseph sent his brothers back to Canaan with the good news that he was alive, he told them, "Don't quarrel on the way!" (Gen. 45:24 NIV). We have Good News: Jesus is alive! Together in Christ let us go tell everyone! But don't quarrel on the way!

On September 11, 2001, our world was changed forever. Radical Islamic terrorists hijacked four airplanes. Two of them were flown into the Twin Towers of the World Trade Center in New York. The third plane hit the Pentagon in Washington, D.C. The fourth plane, United Flight 93, was headed for either the Capitol or the White House when something amazing happened. Some of the passengers made phone calls to loved ones. From them they learned the fate of the other airplanes and realized the intended targets of the terrorists. Somehow they managed to storm the cockpit, resulting in the plane crashing in the quiet countryside of Pennsylvania.

One of those passengers was Thomas E. Burnett, Jr., who was able to call his wife Deena on his cell phone. He told her that he and some other passengers were going to try and stop the hijackers. He said, "I know we're all going to die. But some of us are going to do something about it." Deena later told a reporter from the Los Angeles Times, "I know without a doubt that plane was bound for some landmark and they saved many, many lives more than were lost on that plane."

Another passenger, Todd Beamer, spoke to a GTE phone supervisor. After asking her to recite the Lord's prayer with him, Beamer said to his fellow passengers: "Are you guys ready? Jesus, help me. Let's roll!" The rest is history.

These brave souls came together in a selfless, redemptive manner. No one asked what denomination they belonged to or what another believed or practiced. The crisis was too great. Time was of the essence. Wouldn't it be wonderful if we who call ourselves Christians could unite in an equally selfless, redemptive manner to save those who have been hijacked by Satan and are hurtling for eternal doom?

Brothers and sisters, we are all going to die some day.
But some of us are going to do something about it.
Are you ready?
Jesus, help us.
Together in Christ, let's roll!

EPILOGUE

In all of my reading on the subject of Christian unity there are only a few authors who have made any practical suggestions on how to fulfill our Lord's prayer for unity. This closing section will feature some of their suggestions. Unity cannot be mandated but it is still our mandate. Here are a few plans and programs that I hope will be helpful to all who desire to worship and work "together in Christ."

R.E. Elmore (1878–1968) put forth a seven-point plan in his lesson "Practicing Christian Unity" (*Christian Unity: A Textbook for Promoting the Fulfillment of the Lord's Prayer,* Standard Publishing, 1923). Elmore wrote, "Since the Father wills that we may all be one, since Jesus prays for it, and since the Holy Spirit in the Word points the way, what shall we do about it?" Seven suggestions were offered.

▶ Square your own life, personally, by the word of God. Lay aside the traditions and inventions of men, human names, human forms and prejudices, and be sure that you yourself are walking in the truth. . . . Then you yourself will be one with the Father and the Son, and you will be giving your own fine influence to the fulfillment of the Savior's prayer.

▶ Pray for unity as Jesus prayed on the eve of His crucifixion. . . . We are not following the example of Jesus in this particular as we should. Whenever we pray, let us put in this great petition. When we pray from the heart for Christian unity, we will work to bring it to pass.

▶ Speak against divisions as Paul spoke. . . . Whenever and wherever opportunity presents itself, speak out and condemn sectarianism. What Jesus condemned surely we must condemn.

▶ Be a live advocate of Christian unity. Preach it everywhere. . . . Be enthusiastic. Stir up your friends, and set them on fire for the cause of unity.

▶ Form a chapter of the Christian Unity Fellowship in your community, composed of those who, like yourself, have a sincere desire to see the Master's prayer answered. . . . Meet at regular intervals for prayer for unity, and for conference as to the best means of promoting it.

▶ Arrange for an occasional public union meeting of prayer for Christian unity, and for a frank discussion of the subject. Have someone, thoroughly prepared, give the Bible basis for unity. . . . Have a Christian Unity Fellowship supper for the young people.

▶ In all your efforts keep love and truth inseparably joined together. Love without the truth cannot accomplish permanent or definite results. Truth without love will be mechanical, cold, and unproductive. Shun the party spirit. You are not seeking to make converts to "your church." You are praying and working to enlist all as earnest followers of Jesus only.

James DeForest Murch (1892–1973) and Claude F. Witty (1877–1952) offered a five-point "Approach to Unity" in 1937. The two men had become friends and spent much time in prayer about what they could do to promote unity. They were in perfect agreement that division was a scandal and that even though not many people were calling for unity, the prayer of Jesus demanded that they do something. In *Christians Only* (Standard Publishing, 1962) and *Adventuring for Christ in Changing Times* (Restoration Press, 1973), Murch published the joint initiative, a simple five-point "Approach to Unity."

▶ *Prayer.* Definite private and congregational prayer for unity, seeking the leadership of Christ.

▶ *Survey.* Seeking to determine how much we have in common in faith and practice.

▶ *Friendliness.* Establishing individual friendly relations by exchange of fraternal courtesies and through fellowship meetings.

▶ *Cooperation.* Joint activity in enterprises that will do no violence to personal or group convictions.

> *Study and discussion.* Open-minded study and humble discussion of the things which at present divide us, in order to discover the way to complete a permanent unity.

Thousands of unity-minded people attended these special meetings held in major cities in the United States for a number of years. For a time Murch and Witty coedited a journal on Christian unity. According to Murch, five accomplishments came out of their "Approach to Unity."

> A growing personal acquaintance among brethren.
> A growing knowledge of the current status of the churches involved—their teaching, programs, problems, aims, and accomplishments.
> A frank study and discussion of the obstacles to unity, the impelling motives to it, and possible methods of achieving it.
> Dramatizing and publicizing the five-point approach.
> The creation of a spirit of prayer and surrender to God's will as supremely important requisites to all such endeavors.

Since 1984 a unity meeting has been taking place in various cities of the United States known as the Restoration Forum. Begun by Don DeWelt (1919–1991), Dennis Randall, and others, this annual three-day meeting is geared to bring brethren together for:

> Prayer and worship, including the observance of the Lord's Supper.
> Reaffirming our commitment to Scripture by studying God's word together.
> Respectfully listening to each other and learning more about each other in small group discussions.
> Breaking bread together and enjoying one another's company in fellowship meals.
> Honoring those who have gone before us in similar unity efforts.
> Seeking new ways we can cooperate together as the body of Christ.

Thousands of Christians have attended these meetings. A number of churches that cohosted one of these meetings in their cities sponsored a twenty-four-hour prayer vigil at each church before the meeting began. Offerings have been received for projects as diverse as producing a Christmas day radio special in New York City and helping a new Hispanic congregation in Lexington, Kentucky. People have been ministered to who were preparing to leave for the mission field with the "laying on of hands." Once "A Unity Covenant" was gladly signed by hundreds of people in Lubbock, Texas. The four-point covenant read: "Pledging ourselves to be part of the answer to our Lord's prayer for unity among believers in Christ (and) as disciples of Jesus, we covenant together, by God's grace:

- To share our Lord's passion and urgency for unity among believers as demonstrated in His prayer before going to the cross (John 17:20-26)
- To recognize the importance of unity among ourselves to be able to successfully communicate the gospel to the world (John 13:34,35)
- To turn away from any kind of divisive or factious spirit which is not characteristic of the spirit of Christ (Gal. 5:20)
- To acknowledge that while we may differ in our approach and understanding of what Christian unity requires, such differences should not prevent us from making every effort to do what leads to greater peace and understanding among us (Rom. 14:19)."

In 1999 the Stone-Campbell Dialogue was begun, a series of meetings designed for "charitable and frank dialogue." At the 2000 meeting in Nashville, Tennessee, members of the dialogue issued "A Confession of Sin." The confession stated the members of churches known as the Stone-Campbell movement had been "guilty of dividing the body of Christ in thought, word, and deed" and that this division had "impoverished the whole church of Christ and weakened its mission." The confession sought forgiveness from God and from each other and pledged "to move forward in the service of unity within this family of faith to benefit the whole church and the world."

Ministry Impact began in 2003. At the 2005 event, held in North Richland Hills, Texas, the theme was "Go . . . Together." Planners of the event said, "After one hundred years of talking about unity and praying about unity, Ministry Impact is our opportunity simply to be united. This is not a 'unity' event. It's a united event. It is a one-of-a-kind, once-a-year opportunity for us to come—and GO—together." Designed for church leaders, powerful preaching and cooperative church planting was the emphasis of this latest meeting.

The October 17, 2004, issue of *Christian Standard* carried an article I wrote, "Serving God Together!" I included a sidebar "Unity Starts With 'U'" which is repeated, in part, with a few alterations, here.

- ▶ Get informed. Read each other's books, periodicals, and Web sites.
- ▶ Get acquainted. Start on a friendship level. Friendship will beget fellowship. Invite a fellow believer out for lunch. Few people will bite the hand that picks up the tab.
- ▶ Find common ground. My friend Chris DeWelt says, "I really believe that there are many things we have in common." That which unites us is far greater than that which divides us. Find those areas of agreement and rejoice in them.
- ▶ Work together. Get your people together and paint a house for a widow or clean up a vacant lot. Neighbors will notice, and God will be glorified.
- ▶ Attend a unity event together. The fellowship in the travel time alone may be worth the trip.
- ▶ Stand together. Take your stand together on moral or social issues that affect your community. We do have a common enemy—Satan!
- ▶ Respect each other, even if you may not agree with or understand their position on some issues. Pray together and for each other.
- ▶ Find creative ways to meet together, even worship together. If music is a problem, remember that there's no rule that you have to sing at every service. Why not try an evening meeting just for reading Scripture and praying?
- ▶ Try a joint picnic at a city park. Churches that picnic with each other will not nitpick with each other! I'm amazed at the number of food functions in the book of Acts. They were always "breaking bread" together. Better than breaking heads!

I closed by saying, "We are all going to stand before God some day. I want to be able to say, 'Father, I did my best to answer Your Son's dying prayer—'That they all may be one . . . that the world may believe.'

"I can't do everything, but I can do something!"

Just Like Me

David Faust

Published in *The Lookout*, March 14, 2004
Condensed and used by permission

How marvelous this world would be,
If everyone were just like me!
All debates would quickly end,
And everyone would be my friend.
There'd be no need to disagree
If all would just conform to me.

At church they'd sing my favorite songs
And preach against my favorite wrongs.
They'd start and finish right on time,
And never ask me for a dime.
Why read the Bible through and through,
When I could tell them what to do?

And yet, there's something quite askew
With such a selfish point of view.
And there's a problem I can see
If everyone were just like me.
I guess the trouble's deep within—
The problem is my ugly sin!

If others all were clones of me,
They'd share my eccentricity.
I have my faults, and so do they.
So honestly I now must say,
"How sad and bad this world would be,
If everyone were just like me!"

A higher standard we must find
To make us one in heart and mind:
A model Life, the perfect Lord,
A trusted Book, the Spirit's sword.
Become like me, and hopes are slim.
The greater goal? To be like Him.

A Divided Church

C. A. Boulton

Published in *One Father, One Family*
Alger Fitch, College Press, 1990
Used by permission

The world and the devil can chide us
Because of the names that divide us,
And well may they mock and deride us
   When party names number two hundred.
One Bible is all the Lord gave us,
One Faith all-sufficient to save us,
One Lord who redeemed and forgave us,
   But what of the two hundred names?

While the cynical world now can revel
And mock and deride with the devil,
It isn't all quite on the level—
   The Lord never made the two hundred.
He founded one church to redeem us,
Not two hundred such to blaspheme us,
But thus does the world now esteem us—
   With party names over two hundred.

There's naught in the name, they all tell us,
But party names do make us jealous,
And thousands who think they are zealous
   Are but jealous for some party name.
Why not wear the name of the Master?
The lost world would find Him the faster,
And save us the pain and disaster
   Of jealousy over the name.

And creeds—human creeds—how confusing!
More pathetic, indeed, than amusing.
Two hundred to sift for the choosing
   Of one that is suited to me.
I cannot begin to compare them,
Much less to do aught to repair them

But this I can do: I can spare them
    For the one that the Book has for me.

I endorse it without alteration,
Accept it without reservation—
The simple, divine revelation
    That Jesus the Christ is God's Son.
His name is the creed that is given
To bring us to God and to heaven,
For in Him all our sins are forgiven—
    Because we confess Him, God's Son.

Men's mouthing of creeds may divide us,
And dogmas confuse and misguide us,
But the Book of all books would still guide us
    To the oneness in Christ Jesus' name.
We can speak where the Bible has spoken,
Where silent, leave silence unbroken;
One Church would then stand as a token
    Of Jesus' divine, saving name.

A Better Look at You

Dale V. Knowles

Published in *Meditative Trails*, 1978
Used by permission

When I see you through Jesus' eyes
New, better thoughts in me arise;
His love for me, His mercy, too,
I want bestowed as well on you.

Your sins look different to me
When I behold them as does He;
Repulsive, yes, but not it is
With more longsuffering like His.

I see you as He sees myself,
A soul with whom to share His wealth
Of glory in His Father's place,
Endowed with riches of His grace.

Through Jesus' eyes I see in you
The reason why God sent Him to
His awful death on Calvary,
And that profoundly touches me.

You whom He loves, I should as well;
Whom He desires to save from hell
And have in heaven, I discern
That I for you should likewise yearn.

I can't look through His eyes at you
And not have His compassion, too,
Nor fail to have His gentle care,
And to be gracious and forbear.

When I see you through Jesus' eyes
There's something in my soul that cries
To be to you as good and kind
As He is to this soul of mine.

His eyes are eyes that condescend
With unfeigned fervor of a friend;
He looks on me like that each day,
As I should you the selfsame way.

I would that when you look at me
You would be blest of God to see
Me through the eyes of Jesus, too,
As I have looked through them at you.

RECOMMENDED READING
AND RESOURCES

Allen, C. Leonard. *The Cruciform Church.* Abilene, Texas: ACU Press, 1990.

Baker, William R., ed. *Evangelicalism and the Stone-Campbell Movement.* Downers Grove, Illinois: InterVarsity Press, 2002.

Bream, Harvey C., Jr. *The Church in the Bible and in History* (video). Orlando: Christian Duplications, Inc. 1989. Also available in DVD from Christian Restoration Association, 2005.

Callen, Barry, and James North. *Coming Together in Christ.* Joplin, Missouri: College Press, 1997.

Campbell, Alexander. *Christianity Restored.* Rosemead, California: Old Paths Book Club, 1959.

_____. *The Christian System.* Cincinnati: Standard Publishing, n.d.

Campbell, Thomas. *Declaration and Address.* 1809.

Childers, Jeff W., Douglas A. Foster, and Jack R. Reese. *The Crux of the Matter.* Abilene, Texas: ACU Press, 2000.

DeWelt, Don, ed. *Restoration Forum* (Volumes 5–9), Joplin, Missouri: College Press. 1987–1991.

Elmore, R.E. *Christian Unity.* Cincinnati: Standard Publishing, 1924.

Fife, Robert O. *Celebration of Heritage.* Joplin, Missouri: College Press, 1992.

Fitch, Alger. *One Father, One Family.* Joplin, Missouri: College Press, 1990.

Ford, Harold. *Restoring the Restoration.* Mason, Ohio: Christian Restoration Association, n.d.

Foster, Douglas A. *Will the Cycle Be Unbroken?* Abilene, Texas: ACU Press, 1994.

Foster, Douglas A., and Gary Holloway. *Renewing God's People.* Abilene, Texas: ACU Press, 2001.

Foster, Douglas A., Paul M. Blowers, Anthony L. Dunnavant, and D. Newell Williams. *The Encyclopedia of the Stone-Campbell Movement.* Grand Rapids: Eerdmans, 2004.

Frame, John M. *Evangelical Reunion.* Grand Rapids: Baker Book House, 1991.

Garrett, Leroy. *A Lover's Quarrel.* Abilene, Texas: ACU Press, 2003.

_____. *The Stone-Campbell Movement.* Joplin, Missouri: College Press, 1987 (4th printing).

Garrison, Winfred E. *Christian Unity and Disciples of Christ.* St. Louis: The Bethany Press, 1955.

Goad, Steve Clark. *A Unity Cordial.* Belleville, Ont.: Guardian Books, 2001.

Harrell, David Edwin. *Quest for a Christian America.* Nashville, Tennessee: Disciples of Christ Historical Society, 1966.

Hawley, Monroe. *The Focus of Our Faith.* Nashville, Tennessee: 20th Century Christian, 1985.

_____. *Is Christ Divided?* West Monroe, Louisiana: Howard Publishing, 1992.

Hicks, Olan. *In Search of Peace, Unity, and Truth.* Searcy, Arkansas: Gospel Enterprises, 1984.

_____. *What If We Disagree?* Searcy, Arkansas: Gospel Enterprises, 1994.

Hook, Cecil, ed. *Our Heritage of Unity and Fellowship* (Writings of W. Carl Ketcherside and Leroy Garrett). Beaverton, Oregon: Cecil and Lea Hook Publishing Ministry, 1992.

Humble, Bill, ed. *Light from Above* (video). Nashville, Tennessee: Gospel Advocate Co., 1988.

_____. *Like Fire in Dry Stubble* (video). Nashville, Tennessee: Gospel Advocate Co., 1992.

_____. *Our Restoration Vision* (video). Joplin, Missouri: College Press, 1988.

_____. *The Story of the Restoration.* Houston, Texas: Firm Foundation Publishing House, 1969.

Hunt, Donald G., Burton W. Barber, and James R. McMorrow. *Fellowship, the Issue of Our Times.* Ottumwa, Iowa: Voice of Evangelism Publishers, 1950.

Kershner, Frederick D. *The Restoration Handbook* (4 volumes). Cincinnati: Standard Publishing, 1918.

Ketcherside, W. Carl. *The Works of W. Carl Ketcherside* (12 volumes). Joplin, Missouri: Peace on Earth Ministries, 1997.

Klein, Chuck, executive producer. *The Harvest* (video). Orlando, Florida: Venture Media, 1997.

Lawson, Leroy. *The New Testament Church Then and Now.* Cincinnati: Standard Publishing, 1996.

Leggett, Marshall. *Introduction to the Restoration Ideal.* Cincinnati: Standard Publishing, 1986.

Lemmons, Reuel, and Denny Boultinghouse. *A Decade of Reflection.* Nashville, Tennessee: Image Magazine, 1995.

McBirnie, Steuart William. *The Search for the Early Church.* Wheaton, Illinois: Tyndale House, 1978.

McClung, Floyd. *Father, Make Us One.* London: Kingsway Publications, 1987.

Mills, Dean. *Union on the King's Highway.* Joplin, Missouri: College Press, 1987.

Mouton, Boyce. *These Two Commandments.* Webb City, Missouri: Covenant Publishing, 2004.

Murch, James DeForest. *Adventuring for Christ in Changing Times.* Louisville, Kentucky: Restoration Press, 1973.

_____. *Christians Only.* Cincinnati: Standard Publishing, 1962.

_____. *Cooperation without Compromise.* Grand Rapids: Eerdmans, 1956.

North, James B. *Union in Truth.* Cincinnati: Standard Publishing, 1994.

Olbricht, Thomas N. *Hearing God's Voice.* Abilene, Texas: ACU Press, 1996.

Phillips, Marvin. *Don't Shoot! We May Both Be on the Same Side.* Joplin, Missouri: College Press, 1990.

Phillips, Thomas W. *The Church of Christ* (17th edition). Cincinnati: Standard Publishing, 1943.

Randall, Max Ward. *The Great Awakenings and the Restoration Movement.* Joplin, Missouri: College Press, 1983.

Reese, Jack R. *The Body Broken.* Siloam Springs, Arkansas: Leafwood Publishers, 2005.

Richardson, Robert. *Principles of the Reformation.* Green Forest, Arkansas: New Leaf Books, 2002.

Shannon, Robert C. *Broken Symbols.* Mason, Ohio: Christian Restoration Association, 2003.

Shannon, Robert C., John W. Wade, and Enos E. Dowling. *The Church: A Trilogy.* Mason, Ohio: Christian Restoration Association, 2000.

Shelburne, Gene. *The Quest for Unity.* Siloam Springs, Arkansas: Leafwood Publishers, 2004.

Shelly, Rubel. *I Just Want to Be a Christian.* Nashville, Tennessee: 20th Century Christian, 1984.

Shelly, Rubel, and John O. York. *The Jesus Proposal.* Siloam Springs, Arkansas: Leafwood Publishers, 2003.

Smith, F. LaGard. *Radical Restoration.* Nashville, Tennessee: Cotswold Publishing, 2001.

_____. *Who Is My Brother?* Nashville, Tennessee: Cotswold Publishing, 1997.

Smith, John W.V. *The Quest for Holiness and Unity.* Anderson, Indiana: Warner Press, 1980.

Staton, Knofel. "The Paraphrase of Thomas Campbell's Delaration and Address." *The Compass* (n.d.).

Stone, Barton W. *Last Will and Testament of the Springfield Presbytery.* 1804.

Stone, Sam E. *Simply Christians.* Joplin, Missouri: College Press, 2005.

Sweeney, Z.T., ed. *New Testament Christianity* (3 volumes). Joplin, Missouri: College Press (Restoration Reprint Library), n.d.

Tristano, Richard. *The Origins of the Restoration Movement.* Tupelo, Mississippi: Glenmary Home Missions, 1988.

Walker, Dean. *Adventuring for Christian Unity.* Johnson City, Tennessee: Emmanuel School of Religion, 1992.

Webb, Henry E. *In Search of Christian Unity.* Abilene, Texas: ACU Press, 2003.

Wetzel, C. Robert, ed. *Essays on New Testament Christianity.* Cincinnati: Standard Publishing, 1978.

Winder, Francis J. *That They May Be Won* (5th printing). Louisville, Kentucky: Restoration Press, 1986.

Young, C.A., ed. *Historical Documents Advocating Christian Union.* Joplin, Missouri: College Press, 1985.